5O ways

to support lesbian & gay equality

50
ways
to support
lesbian & gay
equality

. . . .

the complete guide to supporting
family, friends, neighbors—or yourself

Edited by Meredith Maran with Angela Watrous

Inner Ocean Publishing, Inc.
Maui, Hawai'i ✦ San Francisco, California

Inner Ocean Publishing, Inc.
P.O. Box 1239
Makawao, Maui, HI 96768-1239

Cover design by Laura Beers
Book design by Maxine Ressler

PUBLISHER CATALOGING-IN-PUBLICATION DATA
    50 ways to support lesbian and gay equality : the complete guide to supporting family, friends, neighbors—or yourself / edited by Meredith Maran with Angela Watrous—1st ed.—Maui, Hawai'i : Inner Ocean, 2005.
    p. ; cm.
    ISBN: 1-930722-50-8
    1. Gay rights—United States. 2. Lesbian—Legal status, law, etc.—United States. 3. Gays—Legal status, law, etc.—United States. 4. Civil rights—United States. I. Maran, Meredith. II. Watrous, Angela. III. Fifty ways to support lesbian and gay equality.
HQ76.8.U6 F54 2005
323.3/264/0973—dc22   0506

Printed in the United States of America on recycled paper
05 06 07 08 09 10   DATA 10 9 8 7 6 5 4 3 2 1

Distributed by Publishers Group West

For information on promotions, bulk purchases, premiums, or educational use, please contact 866.731.2216 or sales@innerocean.com.

*To my parents: Rita Maran, Sidney Maran,
and Anny Maran.* —Meredith Maran

*To sweet Lilah Rubin, who deserves to grow up
in a world where she can be anything she wants to be,
and love whoever she wants to love.* —Angela Watrous

Contents

Introduction

December 1987. I'm on the phone with my father, making holiday plans. He and my stepmother (who have been married for six years) are inviting my family for Christmas dinner. My father asks what my nine- and seven-year-old sons would like for Christmas gifts and what they'd like to eat. Then he falls silent. "This is a family dinner," he says finally. "So I hope you understand—your girlfriend is not invited."

"*What?*" I gasp. "She *is* my family. She's been raising your grandsons for three years."

"You're in a homosexual relationship," my father says. "You could be with her for a hundred years, and she'd never be part of this family."

I demand to know why his wife is invited when mine isn't. He snaps back that I don't have a wife, and never will. I cry. He yells. I yell back. I hang up on him. He calls me back. I hang up on him again. He writes me a letter, asking if we can meet. I don't answer it. And then my father and I don't speak, and my kids don't see their grandparents, for the next eight years.

During that time, my father and stepmother move to San Francisco. On Gay Pride Days, I march down rainbow flag–lined Market Street with a knot of anger in my heart, imagining my father locked in his apartment, cursing the homosexual hordes.

June 1995. My father has a heart attack. I send him a get-well card. He sends me a thank-you card. I call and apologize to him. He apologizes to me. We meet. We hug, and eight years after we stopped talking, we talk. He tells me that living in San Francisco, meeting gay people everywhere he goes, has helped him see things differently. "I was raised to believe homosexuality was wrong," he says. "That was all I knew. It's hard to change a belief you've held for 65 years." I tell him that I understand. And so my father and I, and my father and his grandsons, begin to get to know each other again. Today, my wife and my kids adore him. And he adores my wife and my kids.

1

Every gay person has a story to tell about coming out to his or her parents. Far too many never get the happy ending my father and I got. What brought my father and me together again was a winning combination. The gay people of San Francisco were brave enough to show themselves to him. And he was brave enough to see gay people—and his daughter— not as he was raised to see us, but as we actually are.

Some people think that to change people's thinking, first we must change the world. Some think that to change the world, we must first change people's thinking. This hard experience with my father taught me that we've got to do both, at the same time, every damn day. It's hard, and scary, and necessary for gay people to be ourselves in a world that is still so unwelcoming. It's hard, and scary, and necessary for straight people to uproot the fears and prejudices that are still so prevalent and powerful within them, and in the world. Understanding came hard to my father and me. But when it came, it saved us. Understanding can save the world, too. But it's not easy to come by.

Hence, the goal of this book: to help lesbian, gay, bisexual, transgendered, questioning, and heterosexual people understand each other across all sorts of misunderstandings and borderlines—while offering everyday, simple ways to do something about it. When a father and daughter understand each other, they're less likely to let anger and prejudice threaten their relationship. When a high school teacher understands *why* it's hurtful to his lesbian, gay, and bi students to hear the word "gay" used as a synonym for "stupid," he's more likely to keep that from happening in his classroom. When an employer understands *how* to make a workplace welcoming to queer as well as heterosexual employees, she can create that more inclusive workplace. When queer people of different backgrounds understand each others' perspectives, they can embody the inclusive world they're working together to build.

Case in point: the first planning meeting for this book. My coeditor, Angela Watrous (age 30), and I (age 52) are sitting in an Oakland coffee shop, talking about the topics the book should cover, the organizations and people we should include, the title the book should have.

"How about *50 Ways to Support Queer Equality*?" Angela says.

"*Queer?*" I say. "I never use that word. Why don't we call it *50 Ways to Support Gay Equality*?"

2

"Gay?" Angela says. "I never use that word."

We look at each other, dismayed. How can we produce a book together when we can't even agree on what to call it—or ourselves? And then it hits us.

"Perfect!" Angela says, and I know just what she means. Our differences in age, terminology, perspective, and politics make us better equipped to do this book together than a pair of coeditors who see eye to eye. Because whatever we choose to call this diverse, lively, argumentative, loving community of ours—gay, queer, or the all-inclusive if unpronounceable LGBT—it's steeped in controversy, inside and out.

When we began working together, Angela and I suspected we'd find more similarities than differences. And sure enough: six months later, Angela and I laugh to hear her talking about the "gay" community and me referring to myself as "queer."

On one point, though, Angela and I (and our 50 contributors, and, I'm guessing, you, dear reader) agreed from the start. We'd like to live in a world in which everyone is treated fairly, and we're not nearly there yet. Understanding alone might not get us to equality, but it's a good way to start the journey.

Consider this book your own personal vehicle (hybrid, of course) with built-in Global Positioning System. Whether you're in my father's situation—a heterosexual parent coming to grips with the news that your child is gay (see "Love Your LGBT Family and Friends")—or mine (see "Come Out, Come Out Wherever You Are"); whether you're the child of a gay parent (see "Value Families Like Mine") or a parent looking for the best way to explain the concept of sexual orientation to your child (see "Talk to Children about LGBT People"), this book will tell you where we are and how to get where we want to be, with tips ranging from the personal ("Buy your child books with gay and lesbian characters") to the political ("Vote in local school board elections").

Toward that end Angela and I have gathered the voices of leaders, activists, writers, and entertainers who write personally and movingly about everything from gay marriage to parenting gay kids; from AIDS to mental health; from being a fabulous drag queen to being a proud gay Latino man. Margaret Cho makes us reconsider our relationship to electoral politics. Judy Shepard writes about losing her son Matthew to hate.

Ben & Jerry's cofounder Jerry Greenfield tells us how to create a queer-friendly workplace. Rebecca Walker asks why we need labels at all.

These questions have never been more apt—nor more urgent. We began this book in the months before the 2004 election, when the rights we'd fought so hard for had become campaign fodder and our very right to love was being debated on the nightly news. In the week after the election, when the contributors' essays were due, I found myself apologizing for bugging them about their deadlines. How could I ask the leaders of Amnesty International USA, Parents & Friends of Lesbians & Gays, the National Gay & Lesbian Task Force to focus on a *book* when we were all still stunned by shock and grief, when our country had just taken a giant step back into the homophobic past, when ten states had just voted to ban gay marriage?

"Don't apologize," award-winning filmmaker Johnny Symons told me. "The election has made me more motivated than ever. And I'm glad to have something to *do*." Several contributors asked for deadline extensions so they could update their essays to reflect post-election realities. Some sent essays from hotel rooms, where they were holed up in emergency meetings. Despite unexpected and pressing demands on their time, every single one of them came through.

In the election aftermath, I had similar conversations with many of my heterosexual friends, family members, and colleagues. They were eager to let me know that the election didn't represent their feelings about gay marriage or gay equality; that they, too felt held hostage by the country's shift to the right. Their reassurances reminded me that the struggle for equality is measured not just by legislation but by changing attitudes and alliances. They reminded me that progress *is* being made (supporting gay civil unions is now the "moderate" position!) and that we gay folks aren't in that struggle alone.

There are millions of people out there—lesbian, gay, bisexual, trans-gendered, and heterosexual parents and teachers, employers and cowork-ers, church members and neighbors—who are all looking for ways to express their love of justice, their abhorrence of bigotry. That's why our contributors, and their suggestions for taking action, address all equality lovers on all sides of the borderlines. All you good people (especially you, Dad): this book's for you.

—*Meredith Maran*

1

....

Start from
the Heart

Opening closed minds is no simple task. That's why we recommend focusing your activism less on changing people's minds and more on changing their hearts. Those who have never met an "out" queer person—not realizing that we're their family members, coworkers, and neighbors—fear who we are and how we love. Sometimes intolerance is so entrenched that even knowing or loving a few openly queer people isn't enough to undo it. It'll take time, and the visibility of respected queer people, to change hearts and minds about who we are, and to convince the world that we deserve equal rights.

While we can—and should—argue for equality until we're rainbow-colored in the face, debating with someone whose mind is made up against equality can be an uphill battle. By laying our hearts on the line and coming out as LGBT people and straight allies in every possible situation, especially in mixed company, we offer others an opportunity to open their own minds. We offer them a chance to put a face, and a heart, to the name—instead of calling us names.

—Angela Watrous

Come Out, Come Out Wherever You Are

. . . .

Candace Gingrich, Youth Outreach Manager, Human Rights Campaign

Some of the most difficult and important decisions in the lives of LGBT people relate to "coming out"—that is, deciding to be open and honest about our sexual orientation or gender expression and identity. Our straight allies must also go through their own version of coming out, proudly claiming LGBT people as their friends and loved ones at the risk of some discomfort or alienation. No one can tell you when or how to come out—whether it's your first time or your one thousandth. Coming out is a personal journey, but one you need not travel alone.

I came out to myself and my family when I was a college student in the 1980s, after spending my teens trying desperately to ignore the feelings I was having. Like so many others, I grew up feeling alone and without resources to help me understand what I was experiencing. But I met a group of incredible women through the women's rugby team on campus. No, they weren't all lesbians, but some were. And being with others who were like me was the final piece of the puzzle falling into place.

My more public coming out happened seven years later, when my brother, Newt, led the "Republican Revolution" and became speaker of the House. In the course of an interview, I was asked if I was gay, and having no reason not to tell the truth, I said, "Yes, I am." And so began my very public second coming-out experience, and a new life as an activist for LGBT equality.

I know that we each have different experiences and that coming out is still a great risk for many LGBT people. But I also know that coming out is a risk worth taking, because it is one of the most powerful things any of us can do. I've yet to meet anyone who regretted the decision to live life truthfully. No one should be denied the right to live fully as a human being because of his or her sexual orientation or gender identity and expression, and it's up to all of us to come out about our desire for LGBT equality.

Polls have shown that people who know someone lesbian or gay are far more likely to support equal rights for all gay people. The same is true for people who know someone bisexual or transgender. So, while coming out may be just one step in the life of a LGBT person, it amounts to a giant leap for all LGBT people.

Coming out isn't a one-step process. We each need to talk to our family members, friends, neighbors, and coworkers every day of our lives. We need to educate the people who know us and love us most—they are our allies in our fight for equality. If we don't tell them about the impact of discrimination on our lives and the lives of our LGBT loved ones, we unfairly deprive them of the chance to stand with us. Whether it's at the family dinner table, the water cooler, the block party, or in the locker room, coming out will help to enact a change that is much bigger and grander than any of us can imagine on our own, and that is how the sands of change shift.

⋛ STEPS FOR EQUALITY ⋚

+ Live your life out and proud, each and every day. HRC (www.hrc.org) has a wealth of resources to help you navigate your coming-out journey, including information on the National Coming Out Project and special information for navigating family and work issues, coming out as transgender, and coming out in communities of color.

+ If you're a straight ally, come out about your LGBT friends and loved ones. Whether you are challenging a stereotype, correcting a misrepresentation, or merely voicing your support for a LGBT friend, relative, or colleague, you can make change happen. Read more tips on "Coming Out as a Straight Ally" at www.hrc.org.

+ Host an event in your hometown for National Coming Out Day, every October 11. It's a great way to invite LGBT and straight friends and family for a day of celebration and education.

Teach Your Loved Ones to
Love You or Lose You

Renate Stendhal, Author, Coach, and Counselor

"Mutti, Pappi," I said in a matter-of-fact voice, "I have to tell you something." I had just arrived on a visit from Paris. I was 26. "I have fallen in love with a woman. I am with women now."

It was a cool spring night in the little German spa town where my parents lived. The temperature in the living room dropped to zero. "You can't be serious!" my mother managed to say and, knowing that I was, started to cry. She had already shouted at me years earlier that I would end up a lesbian. At 17, I had given my heart to a girl in school who never noticed my passion. My mother noticed—she'd felt the intensity of her own exclusion.

But even before I tasted the bittersweet irony of my mother accusing me of being what I longed to be, I had made her suspicious. My first boyfriend had handed me Sartre, Camus, and Genet to read when I was only 14. I had read Genet's *Notre Dame des Fleurs* (a book that shortly afterward was censored in Germany), and the cruel beauty and poetry, the provocative sacredness of passion between men, had touched me to the core. I had longed to share my sexual discovery with my mother, who was still my confidante. "You have to read this book, Mutti," I had urged her. "This is my world!"

On that cool spring night 12 years later, my mother spelled out the nightmare she had lived with ever since she read Jean Genet. "I can see what you will become," she sobbed. "One of those old, lonely women in a bar, sitting there like spiders waiting to drag young women into their net!" What was sacred to me was disgusting to her. We were equally disgusted by each other.

My father, during this scene, had been pursing his lips as if tasting the news and then, as usual, left the conversation to my mother. Later, he appeared in my door and assured me, "Whatever...if it makes you happy." We exchanged a relieved smile, but I had my misgivings. My liberal father, who had grown up in Berlin and been propositioned by gay men in his youth, might amuse himself with a new twist in his fantasies about his daughter's sex life. There was nothing much to be done about this, but I could certainly educate Mutti about the meaning of the word "lesbian."

From then on when I visited, I not only brought my mother my freshly minted feminist worldview, I invited all my lovers home. My sister visited with her family; I claimed the same right to be accompanied by my lesbian lover.

The Christmas photos the first year show my father radiant between me and my part-Vietnamese lover with the disarming, crooked-teeth laugh of a boy-child. My mother looks away from the camera with a pained smile. Perhaps she was having a hard time seeing that exuberant boy-girl at my side as a lonely spider in a bar?

This first Christmas established the pattern of Mutti's education. I set the conditions: You embrace me as a lesbian or you lose me. Her daughter—and her love for her daughter—did not leave her a choice.

⋛ STEPS FOR EQUALITY ⋚

+ If you're in the LGBT tribe, come out to your family in a confident, uncompromising way. Parents are often more capable of unconditional love than we, their children, imagine. Don't add to the drama by crying or cowering or by any expression of guilt. Trust that your parents will get used to it. Trust and expect that you and your partner will receive the same treatment you would if you were in an opposite-sex partnership.

+ If you're a loved one or family member of a LGBT person, be conscious of paying attention to her or his relationships, family, and special events (commitment ceremonies, anniversaries, graduations, promotions, weddings, baby showers, memorials, etc.). Understand that your LGBT loved one deserves equal treatment—in your own home as well as in society at large.

Love Your LGBT Family and Friends

....

Samuel Thoron, National President,
Parents, Families and Friends of Lesbians and Gays, Inc. (PFLAG)

In January 1990, my life changed profoundly. My third child, Liz, then 19, sat me down and told me she was gay. "Are you sure?" I asked her. "Yes, Dad, I'm sure."

"How do you know?"

Her answer was clear and direct: "Dad, how do you know you are heterosexual?" I understood.

It didn't take long for my wife, Julia, and me to understand that this announcement didn't mean that our daughter had changed. In telling us that she is a lesbian woman, she simply provided us with more information about who she really is. She was and still is the same wonderful person we've nurtured and loved from the day she was born. Our love for her hasn't changed one bit.

Still, we needed some help coming to terms with this new information about our daughter. We began attending the meetings of our local chapter of PFLAG (Parents, Families and Friends of Lesbians and Gays, Inc.). Through PFLAG, we received information about what it means to be lesbian, gay, bisexual, or transgender. We received the support we needed.

We soon found ourselves returning the support to others in need. I found that by sharing my story, my experience, I could help other families begin their path toward acceptance of their children. I found that I could do some education as well by taking on speaking assignments. I soon came to realize that support means more than supporting families in pain. It means supporting my child as well.

At one PFLAG event, I realized that, because I'm heterosexual, I can publicly show affection for my chosen partner, the love of my life, and no one will blink. My daughter deserves that same privilege. She and all LGBT people are also entitled to the civil and legal rights of full citizenship. Of course, to bring this about, all we need to do is change the whole world. So let's get to it.

I did not become an advocate overnight. It has been a journey punctuated by moments of decision and opportunity. I found myself speaking out in my workplace when I encountered homophobic slurs. I found myself able to speak in public and on TV, when asked to do so. Each time there was a choice of speaking out or remaining silent, it seemed that I really had no choice. When deciding between what people might think of me and my daughter's freedom and safety, there really is no choice.

My job is to help people to think about what they are saying and doing and the consequences their actions and words have. Silence can only encourage a climate of discrimination, a climate in which violence toward LGBT persons is unchecked, even sanctioned. This is unacceptable.

If I am to support my daughter and those like her, I must advocate for their equal rights. I must come out of my closet as the parent of a lesbian daughter and tell my truth. Advocacy and activism are the logical and necessary extensions of our support for LGBT friends, families, and loved ones.

My challenge to you is to commit to changing the world, one person at a time. Begin with your friends and neighbors, with your colleagues at work. Talk freely and positively about your LGBT loved ones. Speak your truth! Stand up, be counted, and change the world.

≥ **STEPS FOR EQUALITY** ≤

+ Start "coming out" about your LGBT loved one where you are comfortable, and work your way out until you talk about your loved one's life and love interests just as you would if she or he had an opposite-sex partner. As straight allies, we have tremendous opportunities to positively impact how people think about LGBT people.

+ Speak up whenever you hear a homophobic slur or an inappropriate joke. Say something like: "I'm hurt when I hear you say that. You're speaking of my (daughter, friend, brother, etc.)."

+ Join your local chapter of PFLAG (www.pflag.org) and become an active member.

Value Families Like Mine

Nathaniel Obler, Spokesperson,
Children of Lesbians and Gays Everywhere (COLAGE)

As more and more LGBT people replace political activism and bar-hopping with PTA meetings and carpools, a new wave of children with LGBT parents—or "queerspawn"—are changing the face of the American family as well as the queer community.

I was born through donor insemination to two proud and open moms, who recently celebrated their 30th anniversary. In my interactions with others in the queerspawn community, I've met people from all kinds of families: Venezuelan toddlers adopted at birth by gay dads; adults whose parents came out after they left for college; sons of a single, closeted mom in Texas; the daughter of two dads in a long-term relationship in Seattle. No matter how different our backgrounds, whenever I meet other queerspawn, there's a communal bond and a sense of our shared experience. With help from COLAGE (Children of Lesbians and Gays Everywhere) and other organizations, we're uniting in an ever-growing community that is adding a new, younger, and—if I do say so myself—cuter face to the gay community.

That's not to say that our experiences of having LGBT parents are all the same—often they seem worlds apart. A ten-year-old Latino boy whose mom is struggling after a difficult divorce might not have much in common with a white, second-generation (gay child of gay parents) teen. I've always been saddened, if not shocked, at the difference in personal history between a child growing up in New York and one growing up in, say, northern Florida. The experiences can be *exactly* opposite—confidence, community, and pride, compared to confusion, isolation, and shame. Factors such as race, religion, socioeconomic class, geography, the level of tolerance at school, and the particular family situation have a dramatic impact on the experience of growing up with queer parents.

14

The harshness and cruelty of homophobia impact almost all queerspawn to some degree—children of gay parents might experience hurt feelings from slurs and personal attacks, or pressure to feel ashamed of our parents, or fear about coming out to friends, plus anti-gay assaults from society and government. In the worst-case scenarios, some children are teased, ostracized, or even harassed for having gay parents. I've been lucky to have attended liberal schools in a liberal part of the country. I grew up with supportive friends and open-minded teachers, I've had access to an enormous network of kids like me through COLAGE, and best of all, I've had the love and support of parents who enable me to stand up for my family. Yet despite the best efforts of my parents, I've felt the sting of homophobia at summer camps, which has taught me that there are situations when mentioning my two moms can create trouble. This doesn't mean that LGBT people shouldn't be parents, though; it means that homophobia must be addressed personally and politically, to protect our families and give us the freedom to be out and proud about our parents.

One of the most-heard arguments against same-sex marriage is that it will "destroy the American family." But we simply *can't* be destroying the American family when we *are* the American family. While lobbyists and activists spend millions to either promote the gay community or vilify it, "that nice gay family down the street" very well may be the most influential factor in swaying suburban America to support LGBT equality. As more and more queerspawn join soccer teams, sign up for dance classes, win science fairs, and set up lemonade stands, gay America will become inseparably entwined with the rest of America. That could very well be the ultimate goal of this civil rights movement—and it all starts with the sweet face of a smiling child.

⋛ STEPS FOR EQUALITY ⋚

✦ When talking to kids, don't assume they have a mom and a dad. If you've already met their mom, ask them about their "other parent," rather than their dad.

- Support organizations like COLAGE (www.colage.org) and PFLAG (www.pflag.org), which assist family members of LGBT people and help build community.

- If you know a kid with one or more LGBT parents, introduce him or her to COLAGE—we offer a yearly conference for gay families, pen pal matches with other children of gay parents, discussion email lists, and local chapters in almost 30 states.

- If you're gay, think about having kids. I can personally assure you, we're great!

Come Together across Lines of Difference

Tomas Almaguer, Scholar

Coming out is never easy. This is particularly true within communities of color. I didn't come out to my sisters and mother as a Latino gay man until after my father died 15 years ago. As I expected, they were very understanding and accepting. I was, after all, the over-achieving first born and the major success story in our dysfunctional working-class Chicano family. Being ridiculously overeducated—with a Ph.D. from UC Berkeley, no less—had always elevated me in their eyes; none of my eight other siblings went to college. My educational and professional success insulated me from the hostility faced by most gay men who come out in communities of color.

The risks of staking out such a sexual identity are understandable. Historically, family ties and religious affiliations have strengthened communities of color against the racist onslaughts we have endured. The irony is that it is precisely these institutions that have been hostile and uncompromising in denying a sense of dignity and self-respect to an openly gay or lesbian person of color.

In traditional Asian, black, Latino, or Native American communities, conforming and upholding gender expectations around masculinity and femininity are often the real sticking points. Being queer in these communities can be fairly easy if one comports oneself in gender-appropriate ways. A femme lesbian or butch gay man, for example, draws far less attention and animosity than a butch dyke or femme queen of color.

One common response to the dilemma of being queer in a community of color is to shroud oneself in silence: don't ask, don't tell. That was my strategy, and it worked pretty well as long as I wasn't seen wearing one of Selena's hot outfits with coordinated accessories and make-up. But being on the "down low," with its implicit denials, often comes at a great cost. Drugs, risky sexual behavior, self-hatred, and depression are among the many ugly consequences of failing to deal successfully with this conundrum. And that's no surprise, considering that the threat of violence, and even death, often comes with transgressing deeply embedded cultural expectations. One need only recall the horrible murder of Gwen Araujo, the Latino/a transgender teen who was savagely bludgeoned to death, to appreciate the perils of violating both gender and sexual norms in a Latino context.

We need to be vigilant in making space within our communities in which we can be the types of gay men or lesbian women we want to be. A Latino drag queen can defend us against discrimination just as well as a *muy macho* Coors-drinking *vato loco*. It is only when Latino drag queens, along with butch Latina dykes, are embraced as part of the Latino family that we can all come together to change the way we Latinos think about gender and sexual identity. Communities of color have much to defend and protect: our dignity, our pride, our very lives. We can do this more effectively when we are not fragmented and divided along other lines of difference. Asserting who we are, comporting ourselves as we please, and staking out a personal identity as gay or lesbian are big steps—and we need to keep taking them. In the '60s, social-change activists coined a phrase that still captures what we must do: dare to struggle, dare to win.

≩ STEPS FOR EQUALITY ≨

+ If you're an LGBT person of color, come out to your family, friends, and community members (the website www.hrc.org offers a resource guide to help you in this endeavor).

+ If you're an LGBT person, go out of your way to support communities of color against racist acts and laws, and be out when you do so. For example, write letters to the editor that call for support, and name who you are. Or bring a small groups of friends to public marches, rallies, and parades for communities of color and hold signs with slogans such as, "Lesbians for Affirmative Action," or "Gay Men against All Hate Crimes," or "Racism Is a Drag—and Not in the Good Way."

- Support organizations that champion LGBT people of color, their loved ones, and their allies (see Resources).

Cherish the Diversity of the Human Family

Steven Cozza, Cofounder, Scouting for All

When I was around seven years old, I had a Christian camp counselor who became a family friend and a great role model for me. Robert Espindola taught me about morals and family values and God. He also happened to be gay.

I was fortunate to grow up with loving and open-minded parents who cherish the diversity of the human family. They taught me to love and to find the courage to love, even at risk to myself. So when I found out that the Boy Scouts of America (BSA) discriminated against gay youth and adults, I couldn't believe it. I'd been a scout for years, I loved scouting, but I suddenly became very ashamed of being a scout when I learned that my friend Robert and good people like him would not be allowed to be in scouting simply because they were gay.

I could not stay in scouting and remain silent. If I ignored the discrimination of the BSA, then I would not have been true to my own values of social justice. I decided to do the best thing a scout should do and risk it all by standing up against the BSA, the largest and oldest youth organization in this country. I loved scouting and wanted to make the BSA a better program—a program not just for some, but for all to experience and enjoy.

I wrote to government officials and newspaper editors about the fact that the Boy Scouts of America was not following its own scout law when the organization discriminated. Then, when I was 13, my dad and I founded Scouting for All, an activist organization that fights the BSA's discrimination against gay youth, gay adults, and atheists. We advocated for the restoration of the traditionally unbiased values of scouting, as expressed and embodied in the Scout Oath and the Scout Law. We urged the BSA to welcome all youth and adult leaders, regardless of their spiritual beliefs, genders, or sexual orientations.

I was afraid of how the kids at school would react. Some made fun of me, calling me a "fag" or "gay," but I just said, "What's wrong with being gay? Being gay is normal." I got death threats, but they just made me more determined to continue trying to change the policy because they were a sign that there are ignorant people out there who need to be educated. The support of my sister, mom, dad, and friends, and the knowledge that gay kids are being hurt by the rejection of the BSA, have kept me going.

The BSA continues to teach scouts to discriminate. I think people tend to believe something is "normal" or "healthy" if society accepts it. We might think discrimination is okay because institutions and laws say it's okay. We might even accept discrimination against ourselves because we've been taught to accept it. It's important to counter this by remembering that at different points in time, slavery was an accepted practice, women didn't have the right to vote, and Native Americans weren't allowed to be citizens, even though they were here first! Things don't change until individuals find the courage to question unjust laws and institutions. Things don't change until people begin to come together to stand against these social injustices.

⋝ STEPS FOR EQUALITY ⋜

+ Allow yourself to feel the pain of those who are discriminated against. Put yourselves in their shoes. Speak out against and boycott all organizations that discriminate.

+ Sign our petition asking the Boy Scouts of America to rescind its policy of discrimination against gay and atheist youth and adults.

+ Become a member of Scouting for All. Membership donations help us continue our advocacy.

+ Order a copy of the documentary *Scout's Honor,* which tells the story of Scouting for All's activism, for your personal use or for your local school or university, community organization, company, place of worship, or library (go to www.scouts-honor.com).

+ Send a letter to your local scout council and to the BSA national (P.O. Box 152079, Irving, TX 75015-2079) to inform them that you will not have your child join the BSA until it rescinds its policy of discrimination. In the meantime, encourage the children in your life and in your community to participate in alternative youth programs, including the Boys and Girls Club, 4-H, Campfire USA, and Girl Scouts USA. Insist to your congressional representatives that taxpayer money not be used to support the BSA, a discriminatory organization.

2

Speak the Truth

We've all done it at some point. Whispered the word "gay" for fear someone would overhear. Called our partner or a loved one's partner a "friend" for "convenience." Called a woman with an Adam's apple "he." Avoided talking to the kids in our lives about LGBT people, for fear that it might confuse them or, more truthfully, make us uncomfortable. That's why in this section, our contributors entreat all of us to loudly and clearly speak the truth.

Words hold great power, and the way in which we wield them holds even more. Confidently and casually referring to a same-sex partner using the couple's own language (whether "lover," "girlfriend," "boyfriend," or, legal challenges notwithstanding, "husband" or "wife") supports pride and defeats shame. Naming our relationships, saying who we are, validates our very existence and lends us allies in a world filled with far too many antagonists.

When we're unsure what to say, it's a natural inclination to say nothing at all. But silence leads to more uncertainty—and more silence. The invisibility that results from our silence is one of the greatest barriers to LGBT equality. Who's going to feel the need to defend the rights of people who aren't seen, who aren't heard, who aren't there?

—Angela Watrous

Name the One You Love

I t's not easy finding love. I've always found it astounding that so many couples manage to come together, despite the infinite variety of personalities out there. So when I fell in love with a woman who enjoys trashy TV as much as literary fiction, who makes me laugh at myself even in the midst of an argument, and routinely thrills me by revealing new shades of herself, I reveled in my good fortune and set about building a life with her.

Words can't describe who this woman is to me. And therein lies the problem.

Is she my girlfriend? Partner? Lover? Significant other? Wife? When we were first dating, I called her my girlfriend. Now that we live together, share a joint checking account, visit each other's families, and entertain the possibility of growing old together, I generally call her my partner. But what if we do take the plunge and get married? It'll seem anticlimactic (not to mention unromantic) to continue calling her my partner, as if nothing has changed. But to me, "spouse" seems too stuffy and "wife" too culturally loaded.

Let's face it: language is letting us down. Over time, our culture has developed labels signifying the stages of a modern straight relationship: he dates his *girlfriend*, is engaged to his *fiancée*, and is married to his *wife*. But we haven't yet found corresponding ways to describe queer relationships.

While this may all sound like semantics, it impacts the everyday life of queer folks. It's rare for people to take our love at face value, the way they do with affectionate, live-in straight couples. And you might be surprised by how much power the language you use has—it can validate, or it can inflict pain. When strangers or acquaintances refer to my partner as my "friend," I first try to figure out whether they're doing so out of well-intentioned ignorance or uncertainty, or out of punitive intolerance. Either way,

SPEAK THE TRUTH   25

I feel compelled to explain who she is to me for the millionth time, because the only alternative is to be closeted.

Even more damaging is how tempting it can be to hide behind words. Our family members, who are largely supportive, sometimes describe us as "friends" or avoid describing us altogether. I understand that when they don't mention us to their friends and neighbors it's because they're uncomfortable about offending their friends' sensibilities or they're afraid of being rejected, but that doesn't make it any less hurtful. Still, I can relate: when I anticipate intolerance, even I find it tempting to introduce my partner simply by name, leaving it to others to figure out (or not) who she is to me. But each time we avoid naming the truth, we let homophobia win, and we compromise our integrity.

This issue is loaded enough to turn a simple conversation into a landmine. Queer people, too, can step on toes by referring to the love of someone's life with the wrong term. If you're straight, you might feel even more pressure to say the right thing in an effort to show your support. But it's important to forge ahead and have those everyday conversations about our home lives. If you say nothing because you don't know what to say, we'll never come any closer together.

⋛ STEPS FOR EQUALITY ⋜

+ Ask. It's better to say, "Do you have a preference for how I introduce Jill?" than to avoid acknowledging a relationship.

+ Take cues. Listen for the terms people use to describe their relationships, and use those terms when speaking to them or about them. (And if you're queer, use the term you want others to use when you introduce them to your sweetheart.)

+ Be patient. If someone incorrectly describes your relationship, correct them gently and assume their intentions are good.

+ Be out about having queer friends and family. Only together can we effect true social change.

Take on the Pronoun Challenge (But Don't Lose Sleep over It)

Noelle Howey, Author

Fourteen years ago, my father became a woman. In the process, she acquired a stylish new wardrobe. Pumps and flats. Various and sundry plastic surgeries. A new taste for flower arranging. Though it may be difficult to believe, I found none of these changes all that jarring. For me, the big challenges were semantic. Using "she," not "he," "woman," not "man"—and figuring out what in the heck to call her.

Names, like pronouns, were initially a challenge for us. The conundrum might have been solved by defaulting her title to "Mother," as most kids of transsexuals are inclined to do. Call us old-fashioned, but my father and I had little intention of altering the name of our relationship, regardless of peer pressure. I already had a mother, who was more than a bit proprietary about the title. Also, I *had* a father. She might have changed her gender, but that didn't change who originally brought the sperm to the party.

Of course, calling her "Dad" was initially a bit of a mind bender: every image I had of fathers—from a smirking Bill Cosby in geometric sweaters to suburban dads slinging burgers over a grill—was incongruent with this attractive lady in her ultrasuede pantsuit. Father's Day sales featured keyhole saws and paisley ties, not bath beads and personalized bouquets. I didn't want to call my dad "Christine" either, as if she were just any woman I knew. Finally, I settled on the shortened and softened "Da," which wasn't as frontier woodsman-esque as "Pa" or as baggage laden as "Dad," but still felt fatherly all the same. For clarity, though, I still refer to her as my dad or my father when talking to other people; after all, that's who she is.

Despite (or perhaps because of) my struggle with the pronoun issue, I've never been able to find it in myself to go ballistic if other people ask, "So how's your dad? Is *he* doing well?" For me, on the discomfort scale, it doesn't even register. I know that many transgender people and their families feel using the pronoun is an issue of vital importance—that it signifies a full acceptance of the gender change. But we can all tell the difference between a bully who wields the "wrong" pronoun like a weapon and a well-meaning person who slips up. And the way I figure it, at least they care enough about my relationship with my father to ask about her.

What really offends me these days isn't titles or pronouns at all. It's the simplistic assumption that my dad is nothing more than a sum of her newly acquired girly parts. Yes, my dad is female. She is also a fan of vodka martinis and the show *Arrested Development*. Were I to make a list of the things that fascinate me about my father, her gender and sexual orientation (she likes women, by the way) wouldn't even crack the Top Ten. Gender is just a facet of who she is, just as being a woman is only a fraction of *my* identity; it's important, of course, but it's hardly the sole prism through which a person, transsexual or not, should be viewed. It's simply part of the marvelous chemical blend that makes my dad the fantastic, eccentric, one-in-a-million person that she is.

≳ STEPS FOR EQUALITY ≲

✦ Be thoughtful about semantics. Ask people what they—or their relatives—like to be called and which pronouns are appropriate. But don't assume a transgender person is motivated only by her transgender status; what dehumanizes people the most is when they are no longer considered three-dimensional.

✦ Support organizations that promote transgender equality, such as the National Gay and Lesbian Task Force (www.ngltf.org) or the Gender Public Advocacy Coalition (www.gpac.org).

✦ Lobby your congressional representative or senator to take action on issues like gender-based hate crime, harassment, and discrimination in jobs and housing.

Talk to Children about LGBT People: It's Elementary

Debra Chasnoff, Filmmaker and Executive Director,
Women's Educational Media

I was pulling out of our driveway one day when my youngest son, then seven years old, pointed to the rainbow-striped flag hanging over our garage door and asked, "What's that for?"

"Oh, that's a flag celebrating lesbian and gay pride."

"What's a lesbian, Mom?"

I hit the brakes. How could my son not have already known this? His parents are lesbians, and we're completely out of the closet. Half our friends are lesbians. His best friend's parents, Joan and Stacey, are lesbians. We talk about "gay this" or "lesbian that" all the time.

But I guess that somehow I had forgotten to say the words directly to him and explain what they meant.

"A lesbian is a woman who falls in love with another woman instead of with a man."

"Are *you* a lesbian, Mom?"

"Um, yeah."

"Are Joan and Stacey?"

"Yep."

"Oh. Can we get an ice cream after my haircut?"

My son was satisfied that his question was answered. I, however, was humbled to realize that I had failed to do what I'd counseled so many parents and educators to do: use the words "gay" and "lesbian" in everyday conversation with children, and find age-appropriate ways to make sure kids know what these words mean. As the director of the landmark documentary *It's Elementary*, which is all about how educators can address gay issues in schools, I'm seen by many as the queen of talking openly to kids about LGBT issues. Because of the film, I've been vilified by the religious right, appeared on CNN, and I've spoken to hundreds of educators and parents on this highly charged topic. Yet I had somehow skipped over it with my own son!

I know many adults hesitate to go down this path for fear that talking about gay people means that you have to talk about sex. As for myself, I guess I thought my son would have picked up the definition of "lesbian" by osmosis because he was surrounded by lesbians. But sure enough, he, too, needed to have an adult spell it out for him.

Kids often have a much easier time comprehending this topic than grown-ups do. And talking about gay relationships or gay people does not mean talking about gay sex any more than talking about someone's mommy and daddy means talking about heterosexual sex. It's not hard for kids to understand gay relationships or gay parents. They just need a simple explanation.

≥ STEPS FOR EQUALITY ≤

+ Use the words "gay," "lesbian," "bisexual," and "transgender" in a positive way, and explain them to children. Even the youngest children have frequently heard these terms used as "bad" words, often without knowing what they mean.

+ Casually mention the LGBT people your children already know in a neutral but respectful way. You can counter the invisibility that contributes to prejudice by expressing positive feelings about the openly gay or lesbian people in your family, at your child's school, in your community, or in popular culture.

+ If you hear children (or adults, for that matter) call each other "fag" or "gay" as an insult, ask them if they realize how hurtful that is, and give them examples of real people in their lives whom those names hurt.

+ Discuss LGBT issues with your children in the context of current events, such as the fight for marriage equality. Explain both sides of the issue just as you would any other topic, and ask your child what he or she

---

thinks. Teach them to be informed, as well as to think for themselves and to express their thoughts and feelings.

+ Get your children books with gay and lesbian characters and use those as a jumping-off point for discussion. Go to www.glsen.org for recommendations.

+ Watch *It's Elementary* (www.womedia.org) and encourage your kids' teachers to do the same.

+ With your kids, view the documentary *That's a Family!*, in which kids explain what they want others to understand about growing up in all different kinds of families, including those with lesbian or gay parents. Facilitate a respectful but open discussion about the film.

Learn a New Language

Caryn Aviv, Codirector, Mosaic: The National Jewish Center
for Sexual and Gender Diversity

I was in Philadelphia at the first public talk for an anthology I had recently published when an elderly man stood up slowly from one of the back rows, his face purple and contorted in anger. With shaking hands and a trembling voice, he read from a piece of crumpled paper: "Here is what the dictionary says about that word you use all the time. *Queer*: perverted, odd, peculiar. Often used as an epithet in association with homosexuality." He paused and glared at me. The room was so silent I thought everyone might hear my heart pounding. "How can you stand up there and call yourself queer? 'Queer' is what I was called by bullies on the playground. 'Queer' is what I heard when people yelled at me from passing cars. 'Queer' was something that was considered terrible. I want you to know that I'm *not* queer, and I am disgusted that you would even *think* to use this word as something to be proud of, let alone use it as the title of your book."

The panic I felt in front of that expectant audience reminded me of when I first came out to my parents 15 years ago—all sweaty palms, shaky hands, and queasy stomach. The anger in that elderly man's voice reminded me that words and names for LGBT people matter—a lot. They define who we want to be in the world and how we want the world to see us. In the past (and sometimes even today), lawyers, doctors, social workers, religious clergy, and others have used words and names to oppress, pathologize, and humiliate LGBT people. For me and thousands of younger people, "queer" has become a badge of affirmation, or even just an ordinary way to describe ourselves, but there are just as many older LGBT folks who wince at the memory of a word that was used so often to degrade them.

Despite my pounding heart, I took a deep breath and said to the elderly man that some people had reacted just as uncomfortably to the word "Jews," in the title of the anthology; to them, that word felt too impolite or direct. It is precisely this sense of discomfort that can generate important discussion about differences. My goal, I explained, was to get people talking about the power of language to define our world, and to discuss how the meanings of words change—depending on intention, history, and context. I tried to describe how and why many younger people find the word "queer" a compelling and useful term. For me, "queer" symbolizes a big linguistic tent under which lots of people can stand. It's no longer adequate to simply say "lesbian and gay" to describe our movement, which leaves out people who consider themselves bisexual, transgender, questioning, intersex, or straight and supportive allies. Using the word "queer" is an unabashed power grab—taking back words that have been used to oppress us and infusing them with a different, celebratory, inclusive, and sometimes campy political sensibility.

The words we use today to describe our emotional, sexual, and political relationships will undoubtedly sound clunky, goofy, or just plain dated 50 years from now. And that is the beauty of inventing new terms to describe who and what we are. Thinking about how and why we call ourselves what we do heightens our sensitivity to how language shapes our realities, our imagination, and our possibilities.

⇒ STEPS FOR EQUALITY ⇐

+ Learn the history of LGBT people, to know more about how and why people have used certain names and words in the past. An extremely selective list of books about LGBT language and history includes: *Odd Girls and Twilight Lovers* by Lillian Faderman; *Black Like Us* by Dwight McBride; *Stonewall* by Martin Duberman; *Body Alchemy* by Loren Cameron; and *My Gender Workbook* by Kate Bornstein.

+ Respectfully ask people you meet what words they prefer to use to name themselves, and don't assume people use particular words and names based on their age, ethnicity, gender identity, sexual orientation, or country of origin.

Choose Your Words
with *Cuidado*

Daisy Hernández, Editor, *ColorLines*

I was a bad kid, an American brat, the first generation born to a Colombian mom and Cuban dad. Coca-Cola tasted better than my mother's *café con leche*, and I wasn't shy about saying so to my *mami* and my aunties. On my way out of the kitchen, I could feel my auntie's words slap me at the back of my head: *"Qué india."*

Qué india. Translated literally, it means, "What an indigenous woman." But when my aunties said it, they weren't thinking of beautiful brown women. In Colombia and throughout Latin American countries, *una india* is a verbal insult with the implication that you're uncivilized and inferior to white Europeans. So when my aunties called me *una india*, they meant that I was misbehaving, that I wasn't acting right, that I wasn't following the rules. They were, I believe, a little frightened that my behavior was so different from what they had expected.

It didn't help my "india status" when I started dating women.

My aunties stopped talking to me for a year. They were hurt and scared, I imagine, and speaking would have meant acknowledging those feelings. I was actually relieved that we weren't speaking because I didn't know what I would have said. Dating women was exhilarating and frightening, and finding the words to match the experience felt akin to shopping for the perfect pair of jeans: nothing fit.

Having grown up moving between two languages, I knew that words failed me as much as they saved me. The words I knew in Spanish for being gay weren't positive ones. The common one that I heard was *del otro lado*, which literally means you're from "the other side." But I didn't think of myself as being from one side or the other. I wanted a word that described my romantic relationships regardless of whether I was dating a woman, man, or someone who is transgender.

34

By the time my aunties and I did start talking again, I wasn't sure what to call myself. My family didn't speak in English, and the word I had settled on—"queer"—didn't have a good Spanish translation. I found that other women had struggled with this and made words bend to their intentions. I have met women who call themselves dykes, *locas*, boi-crazy lesbians, butches, *mariconas*, *machas*, and—perhaps my favorite—"I'm just that way, you know?"

Everyone struggles with words, straight and queer alike. We hear someone say, "That's so gay," and maybe we stay silent because we think, "Well, they didn't mean it *that* way." When this happens for me and I don't speak, it is usually because I'm afraid to have a confrontation. But words matter, and we have to choose them *con cuidado* (with care). Just think back to the first time you heard the words "cooties" or "you're such a nerd" (or, in my case, *"qué india"*) in grammar school. Words that put gay people down are not just about someone else. They are about all of us.

The word "queer" translates in Spanish to being "rare." But I don't like feeling as if I am an animal on the verge of extinction, so I have settled on *lesbiana* in Spanish because I want to honor in my native language my relationships with women. In English, I use the word "queer." It's a compromise. Words often are.

⋛ STEPS FOR EQUALITY ⋚

+ Speak up when you hear someone making a slur against queer people. Think twice the next time someone says, "That's so gay." Without resorting to a self-righteous tone, let the other person know you're not comfortable with that word being used as an insult.

+ Avoid insults yourself. Sometimes, without thinking about it, we repeat what we hear around us to express our own anger or fear. Next time, if someone offends you, take a deep breath and then speak about what that person did that bothered you. This will keep you focused on what happened, rather than bent on attacking the other person or trying to make her feel bad.

+ Write to newspapers and TV stations when they print or air derogatory stories about the LGBT community.

3

. . . .

Know Your Stuff

LGBT lives are generally excluded from history books and classrooms. Our contributions to society, our stories, and our diverse perspectives are virtually unknown—often even to ourselves. This lack of education keeps us, our allies, and our adversaries from seeing the wonderful complexity of LGBT people and relationships. It deprives us of knowing the courageous people whose shoulders we stand upon: the activists through the ages who have brought us this far and who have set examples that can help get us where we want to be. At a time when what we all need and deserve is a lot more understanding, learning more about LGBT lives past and present will help straight people to grasp the struggles of queer people, and lesbian and gay people to better appreciate the experiences of bisexual and transgendered people.

Here's your chance to know your stuff. Our contributors offer insights into the heterosexism, homophobia, and stereotypes that comprise the foundation of discrimination. Each essay comes complete with concrete tips to help us all address intolerant, ignorant thoughts and deeds. Our contributors also suggest some fun and interesting ways to learn more about queer life, with steps you can take to ensure that others are offered the opportunity to do the same.

—*Angela Watrous*

Acknowledge Heterosexism

Julia Bloch, Managing Editor, *Curve*

I was at a dear friend's wedding on a verdant summer evening. The ceremony was a moving 21st-century blend of tradition and innovation: the bride wore white, yet she walked herself down the aisle. *Both* bride and groom stomped on the glass. Then someone read a prayer wishing that legal marriage would someday be a right held by all LGBT people.

The prayer was beautiful. It was loving and respectful toward me, my partner, and all our straight friends who support us. And it pissed me off.

I was confused. Why was I annoyed instead of grateful that my straight friends had included my struggle for equality in the most sacred ceremony of their relationship?

I knew what I was experiencing wasn't homophobia (though we did hear homophobic comments muttered by some guests who were less than impressed by my friends' inclusivity). My friends hadn't been disrespectful or discriminatory; just the opposite. I was mad because I was tired of the emotional upheaval I felt at straight ceremonies: on the one hand, feeling moved and joyful, and on the other, feeling hurt and discouraged because I have never enjoyed the blanket acceptance and approval my straight friends receive in their committed partnerships.

I was tired of spending money at a wedding registry site my partner and I could never use, because the entire site is designed for "bride and groom," replete with little his-and-hers gendered icons. I was mad because my partner and I can't legally marry due to a system that privileges straight couplehood. I was angry because we live in a straight world where our relationship has to be (lovingly) pitied and rallied around by well-meaning straight friends. Yes, my friends did a beautiful thing that day, but it was still a painful reminder of the prejudiced system that inspired their efforts.

The fact that the prayer needed to be said at all was a result of the heterosexism that pervades our society. The belief in the superiority of heterosexuals or heterosexuality is systemic, much like the ways in which racism and sexism pervade our social customs and institutions. Heterosexism is often more subtle than homophobia: assuming someone's straight unless informed otherwise, calling someone's committed partner a "friend," and listing "mother and father" on school forms instead of "parents" are all common examples. Even for LGBT folks and our allies, it can be easy to share in the larger culture's heterosexist assumptions that children need a mother and a father instead of just loving parents of any gender; that gay men and lesbians shouldn't fight to serve openly in the military, or that legal marriage is a cultural institution that belongs to heterosexual people, regardless of the protections it unequally infers. But if we want to achieve true equality, we must recognize that "what's always been" isn't always what's right and just.

Fighting heterosexism isn't as clear-cut as fighting homophobia: it's a big system of oppression, with lots of permutations. But the first step is learning how to recognize it and agreeing to work on it together. That's exactly what my friends were doing when they included that prayer in their wedding, and while it brought up painful feelings, it also made me feel honored. It reminded me that weddings aren't just an opportunity to celebrate love. They're also the perfect time to challenge our everyday assumptions.

≥ STEPS FOR EQUALITY ≤

+ If you encounter a rigidly gendered wedding-registry site, email the company or organization and demand fair inclusion of all partners. Any time you're asked to fill out a form that asks if you're married or single, or assumes that children could only have a mother and father as their parents, write a letter requesting options for people in same-sex partnerships.

+ If you're straight, try talking about how much you care about the fight for queer equality without prefacing your remarks with "I'm not gay, but...." When you say that, you buy into the heterosexist belief that it's a bad thing to be mistaken for queer.

+ Make allies with people in other movements working on a large scale to fight oppression such as racism and sexism. If you're already working in another social justice group, encourage your fellow members to join the fight for queer equality.

Overcome Everyday Homophobia

Anne Stockwell, Senior Arts and Entertainment Editor, *The Advocate*

In my job I've observed a lot of homophobia that's not directed at me personally. I've witnessed its effects on hundreds, even thousands of lives. Here's what I've learned: homophobia is a shape shifter and a fraud. By definition, it makes no sense: *Webster's* calls homophobia an "irrational fear of, aversion to, or discrimination against homosexuality or homosexuals." Only in a society like ours—which irrationally fears *all* sexuality—would homophobia be taken seriously at all.

When you're first coming out, bursting with happiness that you've finally broken your own code, you think homophobia's just a misconception that you can clear up with a few facts. But homophobia mocks your good intentions. It shifts premises faster than you can refute them. All too often, a homophobic person is talking to you simply so that he can reassure himself that whatever you are, he's different—and whatever you're doing, it's wrong. The more personal truth you offer, the faster he sidesteps. The more you try to find common ground, the more he rejects it. It's crazy-making.

You're having coffee with someone you love, someone you've known for many years. Suddenly the conversation turns to "y'all," meaning "you homosexuals."

"Y'all can say what you want, but two guys together, two women together, that's not natural."

"Yes it is."

"Then how come y'all can't breed?"

"We can."

"Come on, you know what I mean. You don't see that behavior in the animal kingdom."

"Yes you do. In like 300 species."

Pause.

"Well, sure, because an animal will just hop on anything!"

That's homophobia for you. It's so silly it makes no sense. And it's seriously hurtful.

As a queer person, you can respond, but it'll cost you. You can point out that your friend's response is just dumb, but then it's on to dueling Bible quotations and unprovable theories and a real argument that may impair your relationship for good. You can also choose to let it pass—and let your own hurt feelings fester. Then your homophobic friend is likely to end the conversation by saying, "Hey, it doesn't make any difference to me, I love you anyway."

Um, wait a minute, you think. "I love you anyway"? That's not right. He's so uninformed he doesn't know I just forgave him for being uninformed. He doesn't think he's the problem; he thinks *I'm* the problem, and he's doing me a favor by hanging out with me. How long has he felt this way? Always?

Across the table, your homophobic friend is pouring you another cup of coffee. He feels generous. He feels good. You, on the other hand, have left the building. All you're hearing is your own inner dialogue. You've suddenly become one of those people who talk to themselves on the subway.

For all the violence it causes in the world outside, homophobia does its most insidious damage inside you. You question yourself: When otherwise kindly heterosexual people seem to experience queasiness just thinking about you, isn't it just possible that you're as sick as they say? The answer, in case you're wondering, is no.

Want to fight homophobia? Be happy. None of us will ever solve the riddle of our sexuality. It's the gift that unites body and soul. How can we expect to understand something so complex, and why would we even want to?

⇒ STEPS FOR EQUALITY ⇐

+ If you're queer: When dealing with homophobic attitudes, keep your debates about homosexuality in the abstract. If you offer your own

personal experience to prove a point, the argument will become a ref-
erendum on your life.

◆ If you're heterosexual: Question your own conditioning; open your
mind to the possibility that the way you experience the world isn't the
only way to experience it. If you feel uncomfortable or nervous around
gay people, it's better to be honest with yourself about that than to
cite a bunch of bogus science-cum-religion in a desperate attempt to
prove that homosexuality is wrong and to alleviate your uncomfortable
feelings.

Dismantle Stereotypes and Misconceptions

Dulce Reyes Bonilla, Activist

Some of the greatest obstacles to achieving LGBT equality are the misconceptions and stereotypes that so many people have about who we are and what our lives are like. Whenever someone assumes that everyone in a group of people is the same, it dehumanizes those individuals and makes it easier to oppress them. Becoming aware of the assumptions many people have about LGBT people and addressing them in our daily lives and in our social activism will allow us to dismantle these weapons in our battle for equality.

All of the attention around same-sex marriage, for example, has resulted in a widespread misconception that marriage is our *only* concern, and that otherwise we have all the rights we need. My heterosexual folks almost fainted when learning that, particularly in the South and the Midwest, I can still get fired, evicted from school or an apartment, arrested for lewdness, or fatally assaulted—just for being a lesbian. As a working class Latina immigrant, the obstacles to my rights and safety go beyond marriage, but you'd never know it by watching the evening news.

Lately, media portrayals of our community—which have mainly focused on financially secure queers protesting for marriage—have also led to the misconception that only white people are queer. On religious Spanish-language programs, *la amenaza homosexual* my mom is warned about doesn't look anything like the women in my universe of brown/black dyke-dom. Drawing on this false idea that people of color aren't queer, the conservative movement in the United States has started heavily recruiting communities of color to join the fight against LGBT civil rights. This whitening of homosexuality allows conservatives to act out prejudice without appearing racist, and to encourage anti-gay bias in nonwhite ethnic communities without making people feel self-hating, all under the guise of morality.

Other stereotypes about LGBT people have been around even longer—for example, the oft-voiced assumption that same-sex relationships are purely sexual arrangements that no one (including queers themselves) takes seriously. For example, when I told my *mami* that I still held a grudge against an ex who came on to one of my friends while we were together, she admonished: "What did you expect? Things like that *should* come with *your kind of life.*" That's when I realized how low people's expectations can be for queer relationships. The portrayal of infidelity as an occupational hazard of queer life is rampant in the media and in our culture. And just like whiteness and marriage can't be our only faces, "unrestrained sexuality" shouldn't be either. Yes, ours is a movement that can and should support diverse sexual expressions and relationships between consenting adults, whatever that may entail. But the presumption that we are incapable of monogamy perpetuates the idea that our sexuality is out of control and doesn't acknowledge the diversity of relationships within our community.

Fighting the kinds of misconceptions mentioned, as well as stereotypes about our expression of gender, our appearances, and our interests, will go far in countering the biases that make it so easy for people to discriminate against us. By challenging false or simplistic images of LGBT people while openly expressing the realities of our complex lives, we can build the alliances we'll need to achieve equality for all of us—as communities and as individuals.

≥ STEPS FOR EQUALITY ≤

+ Organize LGBT awareness efforts in your home community, especially if you're a person of color. Join a local group and propose that the group adopt LGBT inequality as an issue. For example, I'm currently working at the women's center of the college in my neighborhood, helping develop a "Violence and Hate-Free Zone" campaign to reach students and the surrounding community.

+ Engage in coalition work and support other struggles. For example, Queers for Economic Justice (www.queersforeconomicjustice.org), an active network in New York, organizes around affordable housing, welfare reform, affirmative action, etc.

+ Challenge those who make movies and television shows to portray positive images of LGBT relationships. Become an active member of GLAAD (www.glaad.org) and help put pressure on the media.

Watch Movies about
LGBT Life

Diane Anderson-Minshall, Executive Editor, *Curve*

In the small Texas burg of Azalea Springs, Alex is reunited with Grace, her best friend from high school, while volunteering at the local AIDS hospice. When she finds herself inexplicably attracted to Grace, Alex takes matters into her own hands: she heads to her local video store, where she rents a cavalcade of lesbian films like the quirky, independent *Go Fish* and the romantic classic *Desert Hearts*. Alex, like so many people before her, is trying to learn more about the oft-invisible lives of lesbian and gay people. Except Alex isn't a real woman: she's a fictional character in the comedic queer film *It's in the Water*. The scene rings true, though, because films play a crucial role in the lives of Americans. They entertain and educate us about the issues that preoccupy our country, and they afford us a glimpse of human experiences that are both similar to and different from our own.

LGBT individuals develop relationships with the images we view on screen—in both films and TV shows—and we reconcile these portrayals with, well, real life. Films can show us exactly as we are, representing our experiences as never before. And, just as often, films fall short, self-destructing in clichés and stereotypes.

By seeing well-made queer films, though, parents, friends, and supporters (as well as other gay individuals) can experience just a tiny bit of what our lives are really about. Remember the first time you saw a glimpse of yourself on screen?

✦ Watch LGBT films. If you're straight, invite one of your LGBT loved ones over for a night of videos, snacks, and post-movie discussion (and if you're a LGBT person, do the same for your straight loved ones). Following are my "Ten Must-Watch LGBT Films" to get you started.

Desert Hearts: It's almost 20 years old, but it still sets a standard. A story about finding love—and one's self—in middle age.

Beautiful Thing: A tender, gay, highschool love story set in a London housing project, it tackles class issues, coming out, and fear of violence.

Oranges Are Not the Only Fruit: Based on Jeanette Winterson's semi-autobiographical novel, this film follows a young girl discovering her sexuality amid the hyper-religious fanaticism of her community.

Longtime Companion: One of the first films to deal with the AIDS epidemic, this movie helps audiences grasp the sheer horror of seeing a loved one—or all your loved ones—die an early death.

If These Walls Could Talk 2: A triptych that explores the lesbian baby boom and the early lesbian-feminist movement, this film offers a poignant vignette about an elderly lesbian who, upon her partner's passing, has no lawful right to stay in the house where they made a life together.

Love! Valor! Compassion!: Eight gay men spend a summer together in this charming *Big Chill*–style dramedy.

The Incredibly True Adventures of Two Girls in Love: Teen girls—one black, one white—struggle through a new relationship.

The Wedding Banquet: An Asian gay man marries a woman to throw off his Asian parents, but much goes awry during the wedding.

Boys Don't Cry: A transgendered boy tries to discover his place in the world and meets with violence instead.

Torch Song Trilogy: A Jewish New York drag queen searches for love and respect—especially from his mother—throughout the decades.

✦ Remember, there are literally thousands of films for, by, or about lesbian, gay, bisexual, and transgender individuals—including genderqueer films like *By Hook or By Crook*—that defy categorization. Don't give up on the amazing resource of queer films if you find some of the movies you rent too quirky, independent, sexy, artsy, or boring. Many LGBT people watching some of those films have the same reactions.

✦ Continue to seek out and support LGBT films, especially on opening weekend. Doing so will be informative and entertaining, and it will ensure that queer films get more funding over time (see Resources for more information).

Take a Lesson from History

Terence Kissack, Executive Director,
Gay, Lesbian, Bisexual, Transgender Historical Society

In 1972, Cora Latz met Etta Perkins and fell in love. Cora was 50 and Jewish; Etta was three years younger and African American. "We were a team," Cora would later recall. "We worked together on everything." Two years after meeting, the two women held a modest wedding ceremony. Their bonds deepened when Etta began attending Cora's synagogue, Congregation Beth-Israel Judea. In 1977, Etta converted, eventually learning Hebrew well enough to lead a service. On February 23, 1998, Cora and Etta's rabbi reaffirmed their commitment to each other under a rainbow-colored *chuppa*; the cake featured two brides. Eight months later, Etta passed on, and shortly thereafter Cora joined her.

The story of Cora and Etta would have died with them had a friend not decided that their history was worth preserving. When Cora's room at the Jewish Home for the Aged was being cleared out, her photo albums, which included snapshots of both of her weddings to Etta, were at risk of being lost. Seeing this, Cora and Etta's friend saved the albums and brought them to the GLBT Historical Society, where they were placed in our archives. Cora and Etta's life together is one of thousands of fascinating stories safeguarded by the GLBT Historical Society.

Cora and Etta are a testament to the cultural, social, and political transformations that have occurred over the past half-century. There have always been queer relationships in North America, but it is only since World War II that LGBT people have organized politically, transforming the conditions of our lives and in so doing transforming the communities they live in. The idea of having an African American lesbian lead a service at a conservative synagogue while her European American lover looked on would have been unthinkable before the sexual, gender, and civil rights revolutions of the mid-20th century. As we fight for full equality for LGBT people, it's imperative for us to remember people like Cora and Etta, who, through acts of small and large bravery, carved out lives that were uncompromisingly public, celebratory, and proud. Knowing that history helps us to better understand where we have been and paves the way for the LGBT people who come after us.

Stories like Cora and Etta's help us locate our own lives in a broader historical context. By living so openly, Cora and Etta and people like them have put legal and social equality for LGBT people on the table. By following their example, we can achieve progress that will be built on for generations. Preserving our history is a crucial part of that progress. We must learn from it, pass it along, and safeguard it.

⩾ STEPS FOR EQUALITY ⩽

+ Learn more about LGBT history. Start with John D'Emilio and Estelle Friedman's *Intimate Matters: A History of Sexuality in America* for context, and then read some of the books listed in that book's bibliography. You might also want to pick up a copy of Jonathan Ned Katz's *Gay American History*. Nominate a queer history book as the next title you read in your book group.

+ If you're a parent, see if the textbook your child uses incorporates LGBT history. If it doesn't, you should get in touch with the Gay, Lesbian, and Straight Education Network (www.glsen.org). If you are a college student, ask your teachers and administration to offer courses in LGBT history.

+ Watch LGBT-themed documentaries (see Resources). Write to your local public TV station and let the programmers know that you would like to see more documentaries that explore LGBT culture and life.

+ Help support local queer history projects and archives (see Resources). Become a member, volunteer some time, and make sure that the records of any LGBT organizations you are active in are not lost. As Willie Walker, one of the founders of the GLBT Historical Society, once remarked, "If queer people do not preserve our own history, most of it will simply disappear." We need the help of our straight allies in this endeavor; preserving the history of LGBT people can help all people better understand the progress of our human existence.

Study Something Queer

Arlene Stein, Associate Professor of Sociology, Rutgers University

Many years ago I published a collection of essays on contemporary lesbian lives and went on a speaking tour to get the word out to potential readers. I'll never forget the night I spoke at a coming-out group and a young woman asked me earnestly, "How can I become a lesbian? Is there a book I can read?" I had to chuckle at her question, which suggested that becoming a lesbian was like reading a how-to manual—and I don't mean a sexual one.

At the same time, I knew how important ideas had been to my own coming-out process. My coming out as a lesbian was a sexual thing, to be sure, but it was also much more than that: it was about constructing an identity and joining a culture. When I tried to figure out the meaning of my own desires, I turned to books well before I explored bodies beneath the sheets.

I've always been a bookish kind of girl, so it felt natural to pursue a career in sociology, focusing on women's and queer studies. I'm interested in the role that sexuality plays in our culture—how we use it as a lens to define individuals, and how different groups (such as lesbians and gay men, and the religious right) have mobilized to change social attitudes toward it.

For the past 15 years I've taught the sociology of sexuality at a number of universities. Things have changed a lot during that time. In the mid-1980s, there were no graduate courses on queer studies—even in the San Francisco Bay Area, where I did my graduate work. Instead, I learned what I could from some prominent lesbian and gay intellectuals, many of whom were shut out of the academy, and from some sympathetic professors and other graduate students who shared my interest. When I decided to write a dissertation on lesbian identities, many predicted that it would mean career suicide.

By the time I finished my doctorate in the early 1990s, though, it didn't seem so unusual to be writing about lesbians or even sexuality. I got hired, and eventually tenured, as a professor of sociology. I feel lucky to be a very out lesbian doing work on queer subjects, and to know that I'm not alone. Today, there are many scholars writing books on gay and lesbian subjects, and the field of queer studies is generating fascinating insights about sexuality and culture in general.

Still, progress has been uneven. For every queer studies student at a liberal college or university, there are many students at less progressive institutions who either have no access to such classes or fear that taking them will provoke homophobic reactions from their peers. It's crucial that these courses be offered more widely and that straight students begin taking them in greater numbers, just as white students take ethnic studies courses to gain a greater understanding of, and appreciation for, the people who share their world. We need to work to ensure that the academy incorporates gay and lesbian themes into general courses in subjects such as history, sociology, English literature, and biology.

Occasionally, I still get complaints from straight students in my "Sociology of Gender and Sexuality" course that I spend too much time on queer issues—even though I'm practically the only person in my department who ever mentions the "q word" or discusses the ways in which heterosexuality biases our cultural and historical perceptions. Homosexuality is no longer the deep, dark secret it once was, but a pervasive heterosexism means that the concerns of LGBT students are sometimes still considered exotic at best. As a society we have yet to fully come to terms with the sexual diversity in our midst. That is the great challenge awaiting the emerging field of queer studies.

⋛ STEPS FOR EQUALITY ⋜

+ Make sure that your college, university, or local city college offers courses in queer studies and includes queer content in general courses. If there are none, ask college deans or administrators to explain why.

+ Take a queer-themed class, regardless of your sexual orientation.

+ Visit a bookstore and select a book from the gay/lesbian section.

Walk a Mile in My Heels

Diva Dan, Activist, Artist, and Drag Queen

When I was 11 and tried on my mother's pink high heels for the first time, I had no idea what I was actually stepping into. Twenty-two years later I would become a professional drag queen surrounded by fantastic feather boas, expensive gowns, and enough glitter to bury Pat Robertson. But along with those fabulous things that made me feel fabulous came some decidedly un-fabulous discrimination and ignorance, even within the LGBT community.

Under the glamour of it all lurks a chronic fear of being physically endangered. I am constantly aware of my surroundings and am almost never alone on unfamiliar turf. For every compliment I get, I get twice as many glares and laughs of disgust. I am prepared for this type of humiliation in a heterosexual environment, but it happens just as frequently in the gay community. I truly believe it takes a lot of courage for transgender people to be who they feel they are when society can be so judgmental and cruel.

Because there are more variations of transgender people than there are lipstick colors, it can be hard to get the terms straight (so to speak). Here's a little cheat sheet, though it should be noted there are often heated arguments over which is the more politically correct word or meaning. It's always best to ask the individual which s/he prefers.

Drag queen: typically, a gay man who lives his life as a man but dresses as a woman, usually for special occasions and entertainment purposes. Some drag queens preferred to be called "female impersonators," especially if they're impersonating a celebrity diva. A "drag king" is a born female who dresses in male drag, and a "faux queen" is a born female who dresses in female drag.

Transvestite or **cross dresser:** someone who desires to dress and occasionally act as the opposite sex, but does not identify as gay or wish to actually be the opposite sex. Transvestites never seek sexual reassignment surgery. Male transvestites are usually heterosexual and often married.

Transsexual or **tranny:** an individual who feels that s/he has been born with a body of the wrong gender. A "pre-op transsexual" is an individual preparing for gender reassignment surgery, a "post-op transsexual" has had the surgery, and a "non-op transsexual" is someone who cannot have, or chooses not to have, surgery.

Intersexed individual or **hermaphrodite:** someone born with both male and female reproductive characteristics.

Transgender person or **gender bender:** anyone who does not conform to our culture's stereotypical masculine or feminine behavior or appearance. This would include all the names above.

Whether you believe that being transgender is a choice or that we are born this way, remember: we are all human first and deserve the same respect and dignity as the rest of humankind. We are in a class of our own, but that does not make us freaks, nor does it make us wrong. So the next time you meet someone who is crossing the boundaries of gender, put yourself in our heels (or boots) and see how far you can walk.

⇉ STEPS FOR EQUALITY ⇇

+ Out of courtesy and respect, when someone is portraying the opposite sex, please use the pronouns of the sex s/he is portraying. If the person's gender is questionable, ask the individual. If you accidentally offend someone by using the wrong pronoun, just compassionately apologize and make an effort to correct yourself in the future.

+ If you see a drag queen or tranny alone in social situation, go talk to him or her and offer a compliment.

+ Dress as the opposite sex and go out in public at least once in your life. This will give you a small insight into the difficulties and benefits of being a transgender person.

+ Don't hate us because we're beautiful. Love us because we're fabulous.

section

4

....

Promote True
Family Values

Those who oppose LGBT equality would have society believe that theirs
are the only families in town, and that our families are somehow threatening theirs. Yet with more LGBT people living our lives openly and honestly, there are more queer families than ever. We're parents and stepparents.
We're adult children who are active, loving members of our families of
origin and our families of creation. We're queer youth who deserve the
same unconditional love, safety, and acceptance as all children. We're here,
we're queer, and it's time for us to express *our* family values, for all their
striking similarities to—and glorious differences from—those of the mainstream family unit.

In order to change the popular perception of who we are—which, like
it or not, has a good deal of sway when it comes to strengthening or dimin-
ishing the degree of homophobia and heterosexism that's tolerated in our
world—we need to have a firm grasp of the facts. In this section, contributors explain the truth about our struggles as youth, our abilities as
parents, and our need for support. Not because being queer is in itself so
hard, but because sometimes being queer in a misguided and misinformed
society can dampen the joy of living the lives we most desire.

—*Angela Watrous*

Learn the Facts about Lesbian and Gay Families

Clinton Anderson, Lesbian, Gay, and Bisexual Concerns Officer,
American Psychological Association

Many lesbians and gay men are parents. In the 2000 U.S. Census, 33 percent of female same-sex couple households and 22 percent of male same-sex couple households reported at least one child under the age of 18 living in the home. Despite the significant presence of at least 163,879 households headed by lesbian or gay parents in this country, many American policymakers continue to voice concerns about the soundness of lesbian and gay parents.[1]

There is no scientific basis for concluding that lesbian mothers or gay fathers are unfit parents on the basis of their sexual orientation.[2] While exposure to prejudice and discrimination based on sexual orientation may cause acute distress for lesbian and gay people,[3] there is no reliable evidence that homosexual orientation per se impairs psychological functioning.[4] Research also shows that lesbian and heterosexual women do not take markedly different approaches to child rearing.[5] Members of gay and lesbian couples with children divide the work involved in child care evenly and are generally satisfied with their relationships with their partners, research has shown.[6] In fact, the results of some studies suggest that lesbian mothers' parenting skills may be superior to those of matched heterosexual parents.[7] Overall, the research on lesbian and gay parents suggests that they are as likely as heterosexual parents to provide supportive and healthy environments for their children.[8]

Research also leads us to conclude that sexual identities (including gender identity, gender-role behavior, and sexual orientation) develop in much the same ways among children of lesbian mothers as they do among children of heterosexual parents.[9] Studies of other aspects of personal development (including personality, self-concept, and conduct) similarly reveal few differences between children of lesbian mothers and children of heterosexual parents.[10] (Although the research on gay fathers is less extensive than that on lesbian mothers,[11] the APA equally supports the rights of gay fathers and their children.) Evidence also suggests that children of lesbian and gay parents have normal social relationships with peers and adults.[12]

Generally, children of gay parents appear to be engaged in social life, comfortable interacting with peers, parents, family members, and friends. Fears about children of lesbian or gay parents being sexually abused by adults, ostracized by peers, or isolated in single-sex lesbian or gay communities have received no scientific support. Overall, results of research suggest that the development, adjustment, and well-being of children with lesbian and gay parents do not differ markedly from that of children with heterosexual parents.

The APA supports policy and legislation that promote safe, secure, and nurturing environments for all children.[13] We also have a long-established policy to deplore all public and private discrimination against gay men and lesbians and to urge the repeal of all discriminatory legislation against lesbians and gay men.[14] Discrimination against lesbian and gay parents deprives their children of benefits, rights, and privileges enjoyed by children of heterosexual married couples. Some jurisdictions prohibit gay and lesbian individuals and same-sex couples from adopting children, notwithstanding the great need for adoptive parents.[15] It's time to set the record straight, take a public stance for equality, and stop making public policies and laws based on misconceptions and prejudice.

⇒ STEPS FOR EQUALITY ⇐

+ Join the APA in resolving to oppose any discrimination based on sexual orientation in matters of adoption, child custody and visitation, foster care, and reproductive health services.

+ Help make the facts known. Talk to people you know, and write letters to the editor and to your elected officials explaining the empirical

---

scientific evidence about lesbian and gay parenting and entreating others to lend their support in ending the discrimination that hurts parents and their children.

Put the "I" in Pride

Thea Hillman, Author and Board Member,
Intersex Society of North America

I'm an intersex activist, which means I'm intersex and I'm an activist. Usually when I say this to people, I have to define what "intersex" is. Many people don't know that intersex is someone born with a sex anatomy doctors call "ambiguous genitalia"—genitalia that's not considered "standard" for male or female people. And most people don't know that it's standard procedure in the United States for babies born with unusual-looking genitals to undergo plastic surgery to "normalize" their bodies.

When people learn that our medical establishment is performing genital plastic surgery on babies, they're horrified. And they want to know what they can do to help.

But here's the thing. Intersex is complicated. It encompasses issues of biology, sex, gender, and human rights, just to name a few. Because there's so much shame and secrecy around intersex, the best thing people can do is to talk accurately and openly about the issue.

There are all sorts of environmental, hormonal, genetic, and other variations that can occur in the formation of a person's sex anatomy. Intersex can mean a baby with a small penis or a large clitoris, or even a child with a mixture of so-called masculine and feminine parts (it's impossible to be born with two complete sets). And although these anatomical variations may represent underlying medical concerns, unusual-looking genitals are not themselves a medical concern.

Intersex is primarily a problem of stigma and trauma, not gender. The majority of people born intersex end up identifying as male or female. The best way to raise an intersex child is to assign the child as a boy or girl, without early surgery, based on the best available information about how he or she may identify when she or he is older. Intersex children should be raised with the understanding that they may change their gender later—as should all children.

It's also important to know that while some intersex people are queer, and I include in this term both gender (e.g., transgender) and/or sexual orientation (gay, lesbian, bisexual), many intersex people are heterosexual men or women.

Regardless of the sexual orientation of intersex individuals, intersex itself is definitely a queer issue. Today, all over the country, doctors are determining the sex of intersex babies based on how effectively the genitals will work for heterosexual sex—not on the basis of the child's future happiness or future sexual function. Many of the "sex-assignment surgeries" are fueled by the belief that if left with "abnormal" genitals, a child will end up suicidal or gay. Time after time, though, intersex people who were subjected to early surgery without their consent—or even knowledge, in some cases—have suffered more anguish than those who did not undergo surgery.

While intersex isn't necessarily proof that the gender binary is all wrong, it is proof of our society's obsession with maintaining the gender binary—to the detriment of intersex individuals, as well as anyone who wants to express his or her gender in a way that doesn't fit the current two-gender system.

When I talk to people about intersex, I try to make connections to other issues that are medicalized and pathologized, such as disability and fat. When we educate people about physical, sexual, and social differences, we make more room for all of us to live life powerfully, joyously, and shamelessly.

≳ STEPS FOR EQUALITY ≲

+ Learn more at the websites of intersex advocacy organizations, such as the Intersex Society of North America (www.isna.org), Bodies Like Ours (www.bodieslikeours.org), and Intersex Initiative (www.intersex initiative.org).

+ Talk about the social implications of intersex with others to raise awareness. Clarify that while most intersex people identify as male or female, and while many intersex people are heterosexual, the goal behind

---

performing "normalizing" surgery on children is to create straight people who can perform penetrative, "heterosexual" intercourse.

+ If you run a queer organization, consider carefully before adding "I" to your organization's name or mission. You should be serious about doing advocacy for intersex people, and you should consider having intersex board or staff members.

Join the Village

Johnny Symons, Documentary Filmmaker

When my partner and I decided to venture into parenthood, we anticipated some bumps in the road. Many routes to forming a family just weren't going to work for us—surrogacy was too expensive; international adoption was restricted for gay men; and the old-fashioned way, while fun, was unproductive. Eventually, we chose to adopt children in the California foster care system, where we found social workers and judges supportive of our desire to adopt kids. Thankful to live in such a liberal area of the country, we began life with our two sons.

We soon discovered that opponents of gay parenting were not the only ones who made our new roles challenging. Interactions with well-meaning strangers in the supermarket meant confronting a host of assumptions. "Giving Mom a day off?" asked the guy behind the meat counter.

"Today and every day," I remarked.

"Are they *really* your kids?" someone in line blurted, obviously taking note of the difference in our skin tones.

"Sure are," I replied.

Hoping to find solace in gay neighborhoods, I instead encountered a different lack of consciousness. Restaurants didn't have highchairs. Other diners glared if my kids talked too loudly. Video and magazine stores featured porn prominently in the window, oblivious to the impact it might have on children in the community.

But while resistance came from unexpected quarters, so too did support. One evening in a food court, a woman approached us, gesturing toward our kids enthusiastically. "Are you... are they...?" We nodded slowly.

"Girls!" she called to her two startled young daughters. "These boys have two daddies. Isn't that *fantastic*!"

While I felt a bit like an animal in the zoo, participating in this spontaneous educational effort was very affirming.

Even more surprising was the change we saw in people whom we'd expected to be hostile. Our older son spent his first nine months living with a fundamentalist Christian foster mother named Dora. Initially, she was horrified at the thought of his being adopted by two gay men. But after she got to know us, that all changed. She began speaking up in church about her positive experience with us as gay parents. On a recent Father's Day, she sent us a card on which she'd written, "To the best dads I know."

Dora's evolution is a symbol of hope in a polarized country. With same-sex marriage and adoption increasingly restricted or banned on a statewide level, our ability to form stable families—and ultimately, to parent—is being undermined. Now more than ever, we need our allies to be vocal and active. As gay dads, we may not have a supportive nation, but with a little help from our friends, we can create a safe and accepting village.

⇉ STEPS FOR EQUALITY ⇇

+ Be an ally. Speak up in schools, in places of worship, and in situations where you hear negative comments about gay parenting. Look for teaching moments.

+ Exercise your political muscles. Call your elected representatives and urge them to oppose legislation that bans same-sex marriage or restricts gay adoption or parenting rights. Encourage your friends and family members to do the same.

+ If you're a straight parent, help your kids learn about and appreciate all different kinds of families. Ask your kids' teachers to include units on family diversity. Arrange play dates or get-togethers with kids from alternative families. Expose your children to LGBT books, art, and cultural events.

+ If you're gay, look for ways to make the gay community more inclusive to parents and children. Encourage local café owners to create kid-friendly spaces with children's books and toys. Help your local gay community center make child care available so gay parents can participate in community events.

- Offer your time or money to support organizations that support gay parenting, such as Family Pride Coalition (www.familypride.org), Human Rights Campaign (www.hrc.org/familynet), or COLAGE (www.colage.org).

- If you know gay parents, ask them what you can do in your community or family to ensure that their family is accepted and supported.

- Support gay parenting by becoming a sperm donor or surrogate. If you decide to place a child for adoption, consider choosing gay adoptive parents.

Make It Better for the Next Generation

Kevin Jennings, Founder and Executive Director,
Gay, Lesbian, and Straight Education Network (GLSEN)

Remember high school? Woo-hoo! Good times, eh? Not for me. Like many LGBT people, I remember school as a time when I was scared, confused, and lonely. Being the "school faggot," I often ate lunch alone and ran a daily gauntlet of verbal and physical harassment. I couldn't wait to get the hell out of there.

Schools must be places where all students are provided with a safe space to learn and where young people are taught to value and respect all people, regardless of sexual orientation or gender identity/expression. That's why I founded the Gay, Lesbian, and Straight Education Network (GLSEN), the first national organization whose sole mission is to end anti-LGBT bias in schools. GLSEN grew out of my work as a high school teacher in Concord, Massachusetts, where I helped students start the nation's first-ever Gay-Straight Alliance student club in 1988. Since then, the number of "GSAs" has grown to over 3,000. (There's even one at my old high school back home in North Carolina.) Across America, young people of all sexual orientations and gender identities get together once a week to eat pizza, watch videos, and talk about defeating homophobia. Who'd a thunk it?

But things are hardly "all better." Today, four out of five LGBT students report being routinely verbally, physically, or sexually harassed while at school.[16] This is, no doubt, partly due to the fact that 85 percent of these students attend high schools with no GSA, and 75 percent go to schools in states where they are not included in the state's anti-harassment/anti-discrimination laws.[17]

The effects of this harassment on LGBT teens are heartbreaking. I've talked to a young boy who was literally lassoed in the parking lot of his school by hostile classmates who then tried to drag him from a car before he escaped. I've spoken with a young girl who was told daily by a gang of boys, "Hey, little dyke, someday we're going to f— you until you turn straight." I've held a mom when she told me how her freshman boy had shot himself to death the last day of Christmas break because he couldn't face going back to school and being called "faggot" every day.

And those are just the tip of the iceberg. Witness this email I received from one of the outstanding young people in GLSEN's student leadership program: "When I would report the harassment to the school, they would tell the students, 'Don't do it again,' and say, 'We took care of it.' Things only got worse, so my father has chosen to withdraw me from school. I will enroll in a local community college and get my GED. I really don't wanna leave my school, but then again I don't wanna be tormented either."

Folks, this situation and the many others like it are just wrong, and we, as a society, cannot tolerate it anymore. Too often LGBT youth do not have parents who will fight for them. So we must fight for these students as if they are our own children, and accept nothing less than full equality for them.

> STEPS FOR EQUALITY <

+ Demand equal protections. In 42 states and innumerable local districts, there are no nondiscrimination protections for LGBT students. Contact your state legislator and your local school board and demand that harassment policies be broadened to included sexual orientation and gender identity.

+ Get in touch with your old school and voice your support for LGBT students. If you're an LGBT person, write the principal of your old school or your favorite teacher, tell them what it was like for you to attend their school, and ask them to take action. Check out the GLSEN website (www.glsen.org) and see if your high school has a GSA; if they don't, offer your time or money to help start one.

- ✦ Send your local school librarian some LGBT-themed books.

- ✦ Vote in local school board elections. Show up at candidate nights, ask what they're doing to support LGBT students, and then vote accordingly.

Support LGBT Youth

Craig A. Bowman, Executive Director, National Youth Advocacy Coalition

While LGBT youth have gained significant ground over the past decade, grave threats to their health and safety remain—including higher than average suicide and runaway rates, as well as substance abuse, depression, mental and physical abuse, or harassment. These youth suffer not because of their LGBT identity itself, but because of societal homophobia and discrimination. As adults, it's our responsibility to ensure that all youth—no matter their race, religion, gender, or sexual orientation—grow up in a safe and healthy environment that nurtures their passions, hopes, and dreams.

There are unique stressors and risks that can take a toll on the mental health of LGBT young people. Coming out to family, peers, teachers, and other members of the community can sometimes be a terrifying experience. This challenge is exacerbated when a young person doesn't have LGBT role models or a connection to other LGBT people. And because of homophobia and heterosexism, many LGBT youth struggle silently with overwhelming anxiety as they navigate the complex feelings and emotions around their attraction for someone of the same sex or gender.

Unfortunately, many LGBT young people also face rejection, threats, or verbal and physical abuse from their parents, families, and friends after coming out or "being discovered." Many teens run away or are kicked out of their homes; some end up in "alternative" living arrangements (with a friend, partner, etc.), while others end up on the streets. Almost 40 percent of homeless youth in major U.S. cities are on the streets because of conflicts related to their sexual orientation or gender identity.[18]

Young people often use legal and illegal substances to help them cope with homophobia, discrimination, and concerns about their safety. LGBT youth are twice as likely as their heterosexual peers to drink alcohol, three times more likely to smoke marijuana, and eight times more likely to use crack/cocaine.[19]

With all of these factors in play, it's not surprising that LGBT young people are at an increased risk for depression and other serious mental health issues. According to self-reports, more LGBT youth contemplate suicide than straight young people do, and they are two to three times more likely to attempt suicide than heterosexual adolescents.[20]

The National Youth Advocacy Coalition (NYAC) is committed to ending the stigma associated with being an LGBT adolescent. We are always working to develop new resources and strategies to protect this vulnerable population and to improve their overall mental health. Self-acceptance and self-esteem are critical qualities for all adolescents to cultivate, but LGBT youth are at particular risk for falling short of these vital resources. Adolescents who are struggling with gender issues are especially vulnerable to the harassment and name-calling that can undermine a positive sense of self.

As adults, we have a responsibility to protect young people. Our own journeys should motivate us to get involved directly or indirectly in their lives. Now is the time to stand up and make a difference.

⋝ STEPS FOR EQUALITY ⋜

+ Support your local LGBT youth groups with an investment of time and/or donations. They are working with limited resources and need your support. NYAC (www.nyacyouth.org) maintains a database of contact information for local youth groups around the country.

+ Sign up for NYAC's action list at www.nyacyouth.org to receive email updates about the issues affecting LGBT youth, with steps you can take to improve their lives. Our action alert system makes it easy for you to tell opinion leaders how you believe they should act on LGBT issues.

+ Volunteer to work on a help hotline for LGBT youth.

+ If you suspect that a youth in your life may be LGBT, let them know they are not alone. Even if sharing your own story is not possible, make it clear that you are supportive of LGBT rights with your words and

---

actions. Seeing you stand up for your beliefs will show them that there's someone they can talk to whenever they are ready.

✦ Support a LGBT youth who comes out to you by helping them find a safe and supportive local resource where they can meet others their own age who are also looking for answers. You can find hundreds of these groups on our website (www.nyacyouth.org), as well as in our comprehensive "Youth Connections LGBT Youth Guide."

5

....

Lay Down
the Law

There are millions of LGBT people living in the United States. Yet in a country whose democratic tradition mandates both majority rule and minority rights, we have to demand: Where are our rights? LGBT people spend more than $500 billion a year. We pay taxes. We die defending our country. We contribute in umpteen ways to our society. Yet we're denied the same legal rights enjoyed by our straight counterparts. Where's the liberty and justice for us?

In recent years, the struggle for legalizing same-sex marriage has been at the forefront of efforts to achieve LGBT equality. In part, that's for emotional reasons: many of us want our loving partnerships to be recognized and validated, as they deserve to be. But there's also a practical reason for our pursuit of marriage: legal federal marriage confers more than a thousand rights that would protect our relationships, our children, and our finances. As tax-paying American citizens, we deserve those rights. But bigotry is blocking justice, and not for the first time in our nation's history. That's why our contributors speak about some of the most pressing legal battles we're fighting, and what we can all do to emerge victorious.

—Angela Watrous

Speak of Sexuality

Sue Hyde, Director of Creating Change Conference,
National Gay and Lesbian Task Force

U.S. governments have a long history of interfering with our intimate lives, from banning contraception to outlawing interracial marriages. Sodomy laws that criminalized private, consensual sex between adults were a threat until 2003 because they justified anti-gay laws and policy, including efforts to censor AIDS education materials and separate lesbian parents from their children. Understanding the history of these laws and the way they were defeated can inform the fight for the right to marry, for employment without discrimination, or for the freedom to walk the streets safely.

On June 30, 1986, by a single-vote margin in the case of *Hardwick v. Bowers*, the U.S. Supreme Court upheld sodomy laws, effectively giving states permission to criminalize private, adult, consensual homosexual behavior. In roared the National Gay and Lesbian Task Force. Within weeks, the task force hired a community organizer to lead a project challenging states' sodomy laws. Post-*Hardwick*, we could only fight the laws in state legislatures and state courts, so the Privacy Project would focus on the 25 states that still had these laws.

As the organizer hired to run the Privacy Project, I began working with activist leaders in the 25 states to prove to LGBT communities, friends and allies, state legislators, and the media how we were harmed by sodomy laws. Drawing upon the supportive court briefs in *Hardwick*, we spoke about the goodness of sex and sexuality. I cited research that showed how certain commonplace sexual practices could be considered crimes when performed by two people of the same sex. We asked leaders from organizations of the physically disabled, whose sexual practices were also criminalized, to join our campaigns. We worked with allies from communities of faith who argued that no single denomination's view on homosexuality should set public policy.

During the ensuing 17 years, the task force and our state allies tangled with sodomy laws in state legislatures and state courts, in the media, and in the court of public opinion. I met with leaders all over the country to urge that they organize across their states so that strong and unified communities could effectively challenge the sodomy law. Although only one state, Nevada, repealed its sodomy law through its legislature, the state-by-state organizing to expose the sodomy laws as a cruel cudgel against LGBT people created an atmosphere in which the Supreme Court had to reverse its own decision in *Hardwick*. A promising case made its way to the U.S. Supreme Court, and in June 2003, the Supreme Court overturned all sodomy laws in *Lawrence v. Texas*.

Through it all, the people I worked with were thrilled and appalled, shocked and inspired, by my urgent message: our sexuality is ourselves, and we are good. In the late 1980s, every southern state had a sodomy law, and gay people were only beginning to peep out of the closet, much less engage in political organizing. AIDS was a terrible, secret death sentence. But even in relatively tolerant states like Minnesota and Nevada, discussing sexuality in a legislative forum had never happened. We finally dared to claim our right to be sexual without fear of prosecution.

Post–*Lawrence v. Texas*, some Americans are still more alarmed than encouraged by the mention of sex in civic dialogue. I led a rally to celebrate *Lawrence* in Boston, during which I declared, "Homo sex is *not* a crime!" After the rally, a trusted colleague said that I was "off message" and that we mustn't speak of sexuality because the muddled middle would be afraid to support gay marriage. I laughed because the point of our work isn't that our lives are only about sex, but rather that our sexuality will never again disqualify us from full equality under the law.

≳ STEPS FOR EQUALITY ≲

+ Speak honestly about the harm and hurt of anti-LGBT discrimination, even if success seems very far away. Every mind changed contributes to every gain.

+ Ask for help, and be specific (i.e., speak at this press event, call this legislator, write this letter). With clear guidance, allies will help.

Stay the Course on Marriage

Mary L. Bonauto, Civil Rights Project Director,
Gay & Lesbian Advocates & Defenders (GLAD)

Martin Friedman and John Campbell had been partners for 40 years. After retirement, John, a World War II veteran and a career firefighter, was diagnosed with throat cancer. Martin cared for him around the clock. When John died, his pension died with him because he had no legal spouse to share it with. Martin had to pay taxes on the home they shared—taxes a spouse would not have been required to pay. Not only did Martin lose the love of his life, but because of the pension loss and the tax payments, he also lost his economic security and could no longer afford health insurance. A marriage license legalizing their lifelong partnership would have kept this from happening.

Marriage brings 1,138 federal protections, and hundreds more at the state level. Hospital visitation and medical decision making, pension survivor rights, sick leave and bereavement leave for a spouse, shared Social Security benefits, rights of inheritance—these rights and more come automatically with marriage.

While there's been political heat around the issue of extending marriage rights to same-sex couples, at the heart and soul of this debate are real people who need their government to treat them equally and fairly. Same-sex couples are families, neighbors, coworkers, and members of faiths in nearly every community in this country. No matter how deeply committed or responsible, they are categorically denied relationship recognition and the massive legal protections of marriage. This is not fair, not equal, and not helpful to their families, their children, or anyone else.

Every year, our legal hotline receives urgent pleas for help from LGBT people who need the basic legal protections to which heterosexual people generally have automatic access—sometimes callers have been denied hospital visitation rights; sometimes they've been turned down for family coverage by a health-insurance company. Many of these appeals for help would disappear if the government stopped denying equal marriage rights.

Civil unions and other measures are a step forward to help people with urgent needs. But we can't lose sight of the fact that marriage is the simplest, fairest, and most comprehensive protection for families. We don't need two lines at the Clerk's office. Through past experience, our country has learned that separate is never equal.

Same-sex couples have been marrying in Massachusetts since May 17, 2004. Not a single heterosexual marriage has been hurt because of it. No religious organization has been forced to perform a marriage against its will. All that's different now is that these newly married couples and their children are more secure, with their civil rights protected by their government.

This issue will not be won or lost in a day. In any equality movement, advances and setbacks jog together until fairness pulls ahead. Even now, based on November 2004 election exit polls, the Associated Press reports that 62 percent of voters nationwide say they support same-sex relationship recognition in the form of marriage or civil unions. We must stay the course to make this sentiment a reality.

⋛ STEPS FOR EQUALITY ⋜

+ Get clear about how this issue impacts your life and the lives of LGBT loved ones. If you're an LGBT person, how does being denied marriage rights impact you? If you're straight, how would your life be different if your marriage rights were taken away? To view all of the rights afforded with legal marriage, go to www.glad.org.

+ Sign up for email action lists and support organizations fighting for marriage rights (see Resources).

+ Send a handwritten note, make a phone call, *and* set up an appointment to meet face to face with your elected officials. Send another letter to the editor of your local newspaper. Campaign for pro-equality candidates, even for a day, and take every opportunity to talk to people about this issue. Sharing your personal story, or that of your LGBT loved one, is the only thing that will change hearts and minds.

Protect Queer Reproductive Rights

Leland Traiman, Founder, Rainbow Flag Health Services & Sperm Bank

While other queer civil rights issues have grabbed headlines, there's been little coverage of the nationwide battle over lesbian and gay reproductive rights. Today, when more lesbians and gay men are using reproductive services than ever before, state and national agencies are striving to create policies that could significantly limit our ability to have children.

In 1999, the FDA proposed regulations that would make it illegal for gay men to be anonymous sperm donors, despite the fact that all anonymous donations—for all sperm donors—already are tested, frozen, and then quarantined for six months until the donor is re-tested for HIV. This safeguard is, of course, equally effective regardless of sexual orientation. The new proposed regulation, which was also brought forth by several state agencies, flew in the face of established science and unnecessarily targeted gay men.

The FDA also wanted to make it illegal for health care providers to perform a fresh insemination for anyone except heterosexually intimate partners. This measure would particularly impact lesbians who want to use a donation by a friend or a partner's family member, delaying their efforts to start a family for six months and decreasing their chances of success. (Fresh sperm is 50 percent more effective than frozen sperm, and only 25 percent of men have sperm that survives the freezing process well enough to be used when thawed.) The ban on fresh insemination also discourages women from having their inseminations performed in a clinical setting, where donors of fresh sperm can be tested for HIV and other diseases.

I own and operate the Rainbow Flag Health Services & Sperm Bank, a fertility service that specifically recruits gay donors whose identities are revealed to the mother when the child is three months old. I also perform fresh inseminations for women with known donors (who are not their sexual partners)—a service that few health practitioners offer. Over the past decade, I've fought alongside other lesbian and gay organizations to protect our reproductive rights. Our efforts succeeded in defeating both of the FDA's proposed anti-gay and anti-lesbian regulations. We defeated a similar proposal in California, but we weren't as fortunate in other states. Gay men are barred from becoming anonymous donors in New York and Maryland; while New York allows fresh insemination, the service is difficult to obtain.

The right to reproduce in the way we want to, with whom we want to, is the most fundamental of rights—a right worth fighting for. How we conceive our children is a private family decision; the government should not be making it for us.

> ## ⇉ STEPS FOR EQUALITY ⇇

+ Demand that your doctor, medical group, and health insurance providers offer equal reproductive services and coverage for lesbians and gay men—regardless of whether you yourself will use these services and regardless of your own sexual orientation.

+ If you're a physician or nurse practitioner, provide fresh inseminations from known donors as a part of your practice, and encourage your colleagues to do the same.

+ Go to www.gayspermbank.com to learn more about the reproductive rights of, and options for, lesbians and gay men. If you're a physician or nurse practitioner, contact us and we will teach you how to incorporate inseminations into your practice.

Gain Legal Protection for Gay Families

Kate Kendell, Executive Director, National Center for Lesbian Rights

In the 1980s, when I was living with my former partner and raising our daughter in Utah, my expectations for legal security and protection for my family were very low. I was not a legally recognized parent of our daughter, Emily, and could not be granted such a status in Utah. There was no system for domestic partner recognition; there were no openly gay elected officials; there was no LGBT community center and no gay/straight clubs at any high school. My partner and I knew that if we wanted basic protections (such as hospital visitation rights, the ability to make health care and financial decisions for each other, and guardianship protection for Emily), we would have to save money and do it ourselves with the help of a lawyer. State law would not help us.

Today, the legal status of lesbian and gay couples is vastly more secure than it was then. Truth and love have made inroads. Of course, we are far from receiving protection equal to that enjoyed by our heterosexual counterparts. In many states, it feels as if little progress has been made, especially in the wake of the November 2004 elections, which resulted in some positively toxic laws against LGBT family equality. But our expectations, our hopes, our belief in what is possible will never go back to what they were in the 1980s. The gains we have made in the past 20 years are groundbreaking and touch every LGBT life and every geographic region.

First and foremost there is Massachusetts, where couples can legally marry with all the rights and benefits afforded to any other married couple under state law. In Vermont and California, lesbian and gay couples who enter into a civil union or are registered as domestic partners receive all the legal benefits and responsibilities of married couples under state law. Several other states offer ever-growing legal protections for domestic partners, including New Mexico, Rhode Island, Connecticut, New Jersey, and

Oregon. In over 20 states, lesbian and gay couples can jointly adopt or do step- or second-parent adoptions. A handful of recent cases have recognized the legal status of transgender parents.

Of course there are some dark clouds. In Utah, Florida, Arkansas, and Mississippi, state law or policy prohibits lesbian or gay couples from adopting. In the November 2004 elections, 11 states passed state constitutional amendments prohibiting recognition of same-sex marriage—and possibly even forbidding civil unions or domestic partner protections. In these states, couples may face a specific loss of benefits even if they have attempted to protect themselves. While the precise ramifications of these draconian new laws are not clear, it is particularly crucial for couples in these states to safeguard their rights as much as possible through estate documents like wills or trusts and through private agreements that make clear the couple's intentions in the event of a breakup, hospitalization, or tragedy.

In many ways, we are in the best of times and the worst of times. Our families and relationships enjoy greater protection than ever before. Legal recognition for our relationships is the subject of public debate and attention. We are marrying in many places in the world. More of us are out and joyful and proud than ever before. Yet, even with all our gains, the times do seem fraught with some peril for many. The only real antidotes to the dangers are information and the resolve to empower and protect ourselves.

⋛ STEPS FOR EQUALITY ⋜

+ Read up on the full range of legal protections not afforded to same-sex couples, and use this information when the topic comes up in conversation or when you're writing letters to the editor in favor of legal protections (see the websites www.ngltf.org, www.hrc.org, and www.nclrights.org).

+ If you're a same-sex couple living in a state without domestic partner recognition, make sure you have a will or trust, powers of attorney for health care and finances, a nomination of guardianship (if you live in a state where you cannot do a step- or second-parent adoption), and a co-parenting agreement. Copies of sample documents are available at www.nclrights.org or www.nolopress.com.

+ Personal engagement and involvement have never been more important. Support and volunteer for political candidates who support our lives, write and call your elected representatives, and support the local and national LGBT organizations working for your rights and safety.

Support Parental Rights for Both Parents

....

Emily Doskow and Frederick Hertz, Attorneys and Authors

Consider the following scenario: Nora and Marti had been living together for four years when they decided to raise children together. Nora gave birth to a baby girl, Kelly. Marti didn't legally adopt Kelly, but the two women parented together until Kelly was six, when they separated. They continued to parent cooperatively for another couple of years, and then Nora gradually stopped allowing Marti to have contact with their daughter.

Marti went to court and sought shared custody. She raised every legal argument she could think of, but the court didn't accept any of them. The judges said that because she had no biological connection with Kelly, she was legally a stranger—she was not Kelly's parent, even though she'd mothered Kelly for almost ten years. Marti took the case as far as she could, but she lost at every level. She now has no contact with the child she helped to raise during the child's most tender years.

Unfortunately, this story plays out, with remarkably little variation, all over the country. Parents who have planned for their children and raised them since infancy are shut out of the children's lives because they haven't established a legal parent-child relationship. Some of these parents never got around to establishing a legal relationship with their children, or simply trusted that their partner would never bar them from seeing their children in the event of a breakup. Others live in states that don't permit any kind of adoption by a second parent of the same sex, meaning that protective legal bonds aren't even possible.

It's an unfortunate reality that breakups of same-sex relationships can be just as acrimonious as those of opposite-sex couples. Same-sex parents aren't above fighting over the kids, and in many cases biological or original legal parents have all the law on their side and don't hesitate to use it—even if it means denying a parent-child relationship that they helped to create and foster in happier times.

Of course, the real losers in this worst-case scenario are the kids, who may be deprived of contact with someone they consider a parent. Children don't understand the concept of a "legal parent"—instead, they understand that someone who has fed them, rocked them, kissed their boo-boos, and tucked them in with a bedtime story is suddenly not around anymore. It doesn't take a degree in psychology to know that kids will suffer when a parent they love and trust suddenly disappears from their lives.

Other problems can occur if legal parentage isn't established. Traveling, especially outside of the United States, can be complicated. Procedures designed to prevent kidnapping by non-custodial parents can delay travel if both parents' names are not on the child's birth certificate. For a non-legal parent, getting children covered under their medical care benefits, enrolling them in school, and ensuring custody after the death of the legal parent can all be challenging.

Legal definitions of parentage should establish the rights of a parent who plans for, and intends to raise, a child—and who, in fact, does parent that child for a significant period of time—even if he or she isn't biologically or legally related to the child. Ensuring both parents' legal relationships with their children is truly in the best interests of both children and parents. And the more we win recognition for same-sex relationships, the more likely it is that these parent-child relationships will also be recognized.

> ⋛ **STEPS FOR EQUALITY** ⋚

+ Support equal parental rights. Work for legislation that supports the rights of non-biological, non-legal parents—including the related campaigns for same-sex marriage and domestic partner legislation.

+ Support community ethics. If you know a parent who is considering taking advantage of his or her partner's lack of legal status to cut off a parent-child relationship, encourage your friend to think again. We can

---

each do our part to bring community pressure to bear to protect children's relationships with both their parents.

+ If you have a friend, relative, or coworker who is facing a homophobic custody fight, find a way to lend support and encouragement.

+ Support organizations that work for equal rights for same-sex parents (see Resources).

Abolish Anti-Gay Adoption Laws

Matt Coles, Director, American Civil Liberties Union's
Lesbian and Gay Rights Project

Every year, state lawmakers throughout the country introduce bills that would ban gay people from adopting. Fortunately only three states now have laws that do so: Florida, Mississippi, and Utah.

In 1999, the American Civil Liberties Union (ACLU) filed a federal lawsuit challenging Florida's adoption ban. Each of the four plaintiffs in this case has a unique, touching story that demonstrates the ways in which anti-gay adoption laws not only discriminate against gay people, but also harm the children who need homes most.

One of the plaintiffs in the lawsuit, Steve Lofton, and his partner, Roger Croteau, are raising three foster children from Florida as well as two foster children from Oregon, where they now live. Steve and Roger were asked by the state of Florida to take in three children from the foster care system, all of whom were thought to have HIV. (While the state of Florida bans gay people from adopting, it often relies on gay people to be foster parents.) At the insistence of the state, Steve gave up his job as a nurse to provide full-time care to the three children, whom Steve and Roger raised lovingly as their own. In 1992, after 12 years in Steve and Roger's care, one of the children, Bert, underwent testing that determined that he does not have HIV, making him more "adoptable." At that point the state began trying to remove him from the family he's been with all his life.

After a federal appeals court upheld the ban against gay adoption, the ACLU asked the U.S. Supreme Court to hear an appeal. Unfortunately, the Court declined to hear an appeal in the case. However, Bert is still with his family in Oregon, and the ACLU will do everything in its power to ensure that he stays there.

According to the U.S. Department of Health, there are more than 500,000 children in foster care in this country. Many of these kids are moved from home to home until they reach age 18 and "age out of the system" without ever being placed in a permanent home. Laws that ban gay people from adoption only serve to place unnecessary limits on the number of people willing to adopt these children.

Good adoption practice dictates that all potential adoptive parents, regardless of their sexual orientation, undergo rigorous screening to ensure that they can provide the nurturing and love that every child deserves. This is the type of screening that benefits children—laws that exclude an entire group of people from the pool of adults eligible to adopt do not. Every mainstream child advocacy and mental health organization, including the Child Welfare League of America, the American Academy of Pediatrics, the American Psychiatric Association, and the North American Council on Adoptable Children, oppose excluding gay people from adoption.

Those who seek to ban gay people from adopting often base their opinions on harmful and erroneous stereotypes about gay people. Opponents of gay adoption allege that gay people are child molesters, or mentally unstable, or unable to maintain stable relationships—the same baseless claims that have been used for years to treat gay people as second-class citizens. They also argue that children are inherently better off with a mother and a father, ignoring the decades of social science research showing that gay people are just as capable of being good parents as straight people, and that their children suffer no harmful effects as a result of their sexual orientation.

The ACLU and our allies are using the courts to fight these types of bans. Even thought we've so far been unsuccessful in our challenge to the Florida law, we won't give up. Meanwhile, we need your help in changing public attitudes about this critical issue.

> ⋝ **STEPS FOR EQUALITY** ⋜

+ Learn more about the issue at the ACLU website www.lethimstay.com.

+ Be supportive of gay people raising adopted children. It's important to recognize that today's families come in all shapes, sizes, and configurations.

+ If you are a gay parent, visit www.aclu.org/getequal to learn how to protect your relationship with your child.

+ If you're an LGBT person hoping to adopt, find a gay-friendly adoption agency. Resources are available at www.aclu.org/getequal.

Fight for Workplace Protections

Kevin M. Cathcart, Executive Director,
Lambda Legal Defense & Education Fund

All people deserve to have their work judged by what they do, not by who they are. I know from my conversations with LGBT people around the country that this fundamental right isn't always honored. Kevin Dunbar discovered this the hard way.

A sales clerk at Foot Locker, Kevin was subjected to vicious anti-gay name-calling and physical threats by coworkers. Instead of addressing Kevin's complaints of harassment, the chain transferred him to another location. At the new store, the manager set the tone by telling Kevin, "I don't want your faggot ass in my store," and Kevin's daily nightmare continued.

Kevin was fired after he and others—including a few customers—stepped up to complain about the harassment. One customer had said she became concerned for Kevin's safety when she heard a coworker say, "I will beat his punk ass."

Oddly enough, Foot Locker has a policy that supposedly prohibits sexual orientation discrimination in the workplace. But the policy didn't protect Kevin, because the company didn't enforce it. And because Kevin lives in South Carolina, a state that doesn't explicitly prohibit anti-gay discrimination, he didn't know where to turn. Lambda Legal took Kevin's case to make sure that companies like Foot Locker not only create nondiscrimination policies but also enforce them—and we're happy to report that this case has been successfully resolved. We also launched a national campaign on workplace fairness to educate employees and businesses about their rights and responsibilities. Our message is clear: businesses must judge people by how they do their job, not who they are; employees have the right to a safe and respectful work environment.

Currently, there is no federal law that prohibits discrimination based on sexual orientation or gender identity. Only 16 states, plus the District of Columbia, ban anti-gay discrimination in both private workplaces and public-sector jobs. Only five of those states also prohibit discrimination based on gender identity. So LGBT people in many places have no statewide legal protection against being fired, not being hired or promoted, or otherwise being discriminated against because of their sexual orientation or gender identity.

While there's a long way to go, I'm feeling hopeful. Lambda Legal and other groups are having great success convincing courts that some types of anti-gay discrimination are unlawful under a range of federal and state laws (such as sex discrimination laws, breach of contract laws, and sexual harassment laws). We're also using legal action against high-profile employers like Foot Locker to push corporations to reform their policies.

More and more cities and counties have begun to offer protections to LGBT workers. While public-sector employees often have more protections than those in the private sector, a growing number of private workplaces have created nondiscrimination policies and offer domestic partner benefits; some support LGBT employee groups, which advocate for these rights. Meanwhile, recent polls show that the vast majority of Americans think LGBT people should be free of harassment and discrimination at work. All of this has caused employers across the country to realize that attracting high-quality employees and keeping them happy means creating a fair and open environment for LGBT people.

≥ STEPS FOR EQUALITY ≤

+ Come out at work. The more we talk about our lives (or the lives of our LGBT friends and family) at work, the easier it becomes for our coworkers and managers to know and accept LGBT people for who we are.

+ Join an LGBT employee group. If your company doesn't already have one, get a few coworkers together and start one. For information on starting an LGBT employee group, see Lambda Legal's tool kit, *Out at Work: A Guide for LGBT Employees* (www.lambdalegal.org/cgi-bin/iowa/documents/record?record=1493).

- If your company doesn't have a nondiscrimination policy, take steps to create one; if a policy exists that doesn't include provisions for LGBT workers, fight to get those protections added. For help creating a nondiscrimination policy, see *Out at Work: A Guide for LGBT Employees* at the URL listed in the previous bullet.

- Join "Blow the Whistle on Workplace Discrimination," Lambda Legal's nationwide campaign to protect LGBT employees (www.lambdalegal.org). Participate in timely Action Alerts and help spread the work about Lambda Legal's employment-fairness cases and initiatives.

Address Transgender Rights

Christopher Daley, Director, Transgender Law Center

Despite unprecedented advances in transgender civil rights over the past decade, transgender people continue to face significant barriers to full and free inclusion in society. Transgender people and their families experience shocking rates of employment discrimination, myriad obstacles in procuring health care services and insurance, frequent harassment and assault by police officers, alienation from educational environments and opportunities, difficulties creating legally recognized family relationships, and unique barriers to obtaining legal immigration status.[1] The consequences of these challenges are clear: high rates of under-employment and poverty, and compromised physical health. Less measurable, but no less harmful, are the secondary effects: due to these kinds of oppressive policies and beliefs, some transgender people find themselves with low self-esteem and high rates of depression and anxiety linked to pervasive concerns about their physical and/or economic security.

In response to—and, in many cases, despite—these challenges, more and more transgender people are banding together in attempts to dismantle these barriers to equality. Local, regional, and national efforts are underway to pass and enforce protective laws and policies, to create and present sensitivity trainings, and to draw attention to transgender issues through marches, rallies, and conferences. And, as in any movement for social justice, those of us who are non-transgender have the ability and responsibility to make the world a place in which each of us can fully and freely express our gender identity.

The first step to becoming an ally, if you haven't already taken it, is to realize that even non-transgender people have a gender identity (which is sometimes defined as our internal understanding of our own gender). Those of us who are not transgender often don't realize that we have a gender identity simply because the sex we are assigned at birth corresponds to our gender identity (for example, I was identified as male at birth and have a male identity). By recognizing our own gender identity, we can see how much easier it is to navigate in our society if there is no difference between the sex we're assigned and the gender we feel we are—and we can also begin to understand the changes that we all must make so that transgender people can feel comfortable expressing their own gender identity.

The second step is to advocate for policies and practices that clearly support and respect transgender people. Regrettably, nearly every institution in the United States could benefit from some kind of advocacy aimed at making it safer for transgender people. The places where you work, shop, worship, socialize, volunteer, and/or receive services are all places where your advocacy could make a difference.

Likely, somewhere in your local area there's an organization working on transgender issues. As allies, it is particularly important that we work in collaboration with such organizations to make sure our efforts fit into their overall strategy—no doubt, they have spent a lot of time thinking about the best ways to create social change that benefits transgender people. As a non-transgender person who has been doing transgender civil rights work for more than three years, I can attest to the warm receptions I've received in the transgender community. By remembering that such community acceptance should never be mistaken for membership, and by collaborating with a diverse pool of community members in your support of LGBT equality, you can take the first important steps to becoming a transgender ally.

⇒ STEPS FOR EQUALITY ⇐

+ Take the initiative to educate yourself as much as possible (see Resources). One tenet of being a good ally is not taking up too much time asking questions that you can answer for yourself through basic self-education.

+ Don't assume that any one transgender person speaks for the community, or expect every transgender person to be an expert on any or all transgender issues.

---

* Incorporate transgender issues into your ongoing social justice work or volunteerism.

* Adopt a transgender organization or organizations and become a regular donor (see Resources). Due to many of the societal barriers mentioned above, transgender organizations are generally not able to raise enough funds within the community to survive and thrive.

Demand Immigration Equality

Victoria Neilson, Legal Director, Immigration Equality

Wendy, a U.S. citizen, fell in love with Belinda while vacationing in Belinda's native Wales. After trying to maintain a long-distance relationship, Belinda was able to secure a work visa to come to the United States and be with Wendy. The couple established a community of friends, and even married in San Francisco last February, but they face the unhappy certainty that Belinda's visa will expire next year. At that point their only option will be to leave behind their family and friends and relocate to Wales. Terrible as this situation is, they are among the "lucky" bi-national couples who have the option to emigrate to Belinda's country, which recognizes same-sex relationships and grants its citizens the right to petition for legal permanent residence for their foreign partners.

Of the more than 1,100 rights that marriage confers upon couples, it is difficult to imagine any right more fundamental than the right to be in the same country with one's partner. Yet every day, same-sex partners must make the heart-rending decision to give up either the love of their lives or the country they love, simply because one was born in the United States and the other was not. Under current immigration law, there is no mechanism for a U.S. citizen or legal permanent resident to sponsor his or her partner, no matter how committed their relationship or how long they have been together. While 16 countries provide immigration benefits for same-sex partners of their citizens, the United States lags woefully behind.

Even couples who have lawfully wed in jurisdictions recognizing gay marriages, such as Massachusetts or Canada, will be unable to obtain immigration benefits based on such marriages. Immigration law in the United States is entirely federal, and the 1996 Defense of Marriage Act defines marriage for federal purposes as the union between a man and a woman. Thus, any immigration application based on a same-sex marriage will be denied, and the foreign partner could be at risk for deportation following the denial. Making matters even worse, many temporary visas to the United States, such as tourist visas and student visas, require the foreign national to prove continually that he or she does not intend to remain in the United States permanently. This means that disclosing a long-term relationship with an American can actually put a foreign visitor at risk for losing a U.S. visa.

As bleak a landscape as this is, there is hope on the horizon. In 2000, Jerrold Nadler introduced the Permanent Partners Immigration Act (PPIA) in the House (H.R. 832) and in 2003 Senator Patrick Leahy introduced a companion bill in the Senate (S. 1510). The bill is set to be re-introduced in the current Congress in May 2005, perhaps under a different name. If passed, the bill would add the words "permanent partner" to the Immigration and Nationality Act wherever the word "spouse" currently appears. As with heterosexual couples, permanent partners would be required to prove that they are financially interdependent and that their relationship is bona fide.

With a climate in Washington that has been hostile to both immigrants' rights and lesbian and gay rights, the permanent partner bill faces an uphill battle. But it continues to gain support and new cosponsors. Our greatest strength in the struggle for the passage of the bill is the simplicity of our demand—immigration equality. All we ask for is the same right that opposite-sex couples enjoy: to be together with the partners we love in the country we love.

⇉ STEPS FOR EQUALITY ⇇

+ Organize. Contact your local chapter of Immigration Equality (or get information on starting your own chapter) to see where you can fit into this grassroots movement. See www.immigrationequality.org.

+ Advocate. Find out whether your senators and congressperson support the PPIA (see www.hrc.org for information on congressional cosponsors). If they already support the PPIA, thank them and ask them to take a more active leadership role. If they don't, let them know why this issue is so important, and make an appointment to speak with them further.

✦ Educate. Keep telling your stories. Write an op-ed piece for your local newspaper. The stories of bi-national couples are love stories, and the more people hear the human side of the discriminatory immigration law, the more likely it is that we will be able to bring about change.

Ask. Tell.

C. Dixon Osburn, Executive Director,
Servicemembers Legal Defense Network

Every day, the Pentagon fires two to three people for being gay. Arabic linguists, Green Berets, Black Hawk pilots, and other skilled men and women have been discharged simply because of their sexual orientation. According to the Department of Defense, in its first decade, the infamous "Don't Ask, Don't Tell" policy has led to the exodus of nearly 10,000 patriotic Americans from our armed forces.[2]

During that same decade, Servicemembers Legal Defense Network (SLDN) has answered more than 6,000 calls for assistance. Our attorneys are often the only resource available to men and women targeted under the military's gay ban.

When Dr. Monica Hill lost her job because she asked for a deferment to care for her dying partner, she turned to SLDN for help. When Patricia Kutteles learned her son Barry had been killed by his fellow soldiers in a vicious anti-gay hate crime, she turned to SLDN for help. When former airman Lauren Brown's car was torched and her life was threatened, she too turned to SLDN for help.

LGBT military personnel face a hostile, sometimes deadly work environment. SLDN's clients report encountering daily anti-gay harassment, threats, and intimidation. By the Department of Defense's own admission,[3] anti-gay animus is rampant in the armed forces. "Fag" and "dyke" are as commonplace as "sir" and "ma'am" in today's military.

There is no question that most gay Americans would be outraged if our local Wal-Mart or Target were harassing, firing, and threatening gay and lesbian employees. Yet our nation's largest employer, the U.S. military, does so under the sanction of law. "Don't Ask, Don't Tell" is the only law at the federal, state, or local level that mandates firing a gay employee. Today, the military can imprison American service personnel who are in same-sex relationships for up to five years.

Lesbian and gay Americans from every community, military or civilian, should be moved to action. Like most Americans, lesbian and gay citizens join the armed forces because they are courageous and patriotic. Like many Americans, they join for economic and educational opportunity. They often look to the military as a chance to escape a hostile home life. They see an opportunity to travel, learn, and begin a career. Few believe their own government could treat them as second-class citizens.

Consider former Staff Sergeant Leonard Peacock's experience, in his own words: "I wanted to serve my country, just like my father had. I got to my truck one day to see black stickers spelling out 'fag,' 'rainbow warrior,' 'gay,' and other epithets on my windshield. Being mistreated by so many other soldiers and being discharged from the military just because of one's sexual orientation is discrimination—plain and simple."

The opportunity to contribute—the freedom to serve—is in the best interests of our nation, our people, and our liberty. Gay Americans have contributed to our nation since the American Revolution. Today, the U.S. military has the opportunity to join forces with our strongest military allies in supporting its LGBT service members. Great Britain, Israel, Australia, Canada and more than 20 other nations now welcome openly gay personnel. Our troops fight alongside openly gay allied troops throughout the world. Not one American service member has reported any difficulty in working beside those allied forces. According to a study conducted by the Urban Institute in October 2003, there are 65,000 lesbian and gay patriots serving today. One million gay veterans have served before them, and their victories are proof that patriotism knows no sexual orientation.

⇒ STEPS FOR EQUALITY ⇐

+ Log on to www.lifttheban.org and sign a petition asking Congress to repeal "Don't Ask, Don't Tell" once and for all.

+ Visit www.sldn.org for more information on the military's gay ban, SLDN's strategic plan to end "Don't Ask, Don't Tell," and activist events in your community.

+ Write to the Secretary of Defense (www.defenselink.mil) and ask the Pentagon to curb anti-gay harassment and allow troops to serve openly.

+ Submit your story about being a lesbian, gay, bisexual, or transgender veteran to "Documenting Courage." For more information, visit SLDN online or send an email (sldn@sldn.org).

+ Tell your elected representatives that you support LGBT troops. To locate your members of Congress, visit www.house.gov and www.senate.gov.

Engage in the Politics of Equality

Keely Savoie, Journalist

I watched the 2004 presidential election campaign from my progressive neighborhood—where rainbow flags festoon every third house, and every other car sports "Wage Peace" stickers—with a growing feeling of disconnectedness and despair. Each candidate's platform was steeped in homophobia; the macho swagger of politicians terrified of being tarred as girly-men had infiltrated the public discourse, and the time for nuanced analysis of social and political policies was over. "Moral values" had become the catchphrase of the season.

But for gays and lesbians and our friends and families, all that talk about "compassionate conservatism," the "sanctity of marriage," and "protecting the family" meant one thing—that the gay rights movement, the bastard child of civil rights and sexual liberation, had been kicked out of the nest, and our very survival as a movement was in question.

Still, like millions of other gays and lesbians, I got up early and stood in line to vote for a man who openly disavowed my right to marry my girlfriend, for someone who had choked on the word "lesbian" like a *Fear Factor* contestant gagging on a mouthful of maggots. Later, watching the returns with my girlfriend from the safety of our living room, I felt like I'd been had. In the aftermath, even the dwindling ranks of progressive politicians were urging a turn toward socially conservative views in the interest of winning future elections.

How do we continue to participate in a system that is so bent on our exclusion? Gay and lesbian issues are so often sacrificed like useless pawns in the game of national politics; in every election, it seems, we are handed a lose-lose choice and told to make our pick. When state legislatures write intolerance into constitutions, when hate-crime bills are gutted or not enforced, and when we're denied the ability to exercise all the vital rights that heterosexual couples take for granted, it can seem as if all the work we've done has come to nothing. Ideals of social equality and economic justice are branded "elitist," and the party of progressives tacks farther rightward in order to appease the ever-elusive swing voter, leaving the rest of us dangling.

No wonder so many of us walk away.

It is all too tempting to buy into to idea that, in the words of my political nemeses and disconsolate friends alike, "America is not ready for gay marriage," by which they mean "gay rights." But I don't believe it. I believe that politicians lack the incentive to embrace socially progressive platforms because they are afraid to stand alone on such an explosive issue. But even while some state legislatures were preparing to ban gay marriage, the Massachusetts Supreme Court declared that allowing same-sex marriage was not only permitted by the state constitution, but required, and mayors from around the country flung open the doors to city halls—however briefly—to wed gay couples. The country is ready for us to have equal civil rights. We just need to support the brave politicians who have dared to embrace us, and put our weight behind others who promise to do the same.

≥ STEPS FOR EQUALITY ≤

+ Start local. Get involved in your neighborhood politics and your local elections. Get to know who is running. Make a point of asking them their positions on gay issues—and tell them yours.

+ Vote in primaries. Whether or not your candidate wins, the more people who vote for gay-friendly platforms, the louder the message to party leadership.

+ Make it personal. Talking to family and friends about your concerns puts a face on the movement. Explain in personal, heartfelt terms why voting for LGBT equality is important to you and your family.

+ Inform yourself. The website www.marriageequality.org features up-to-date facts about gay marriage and useful information to increase your own knowledge or to help open someone else's mind.

+ Get to know your community resources. The National Gay and Lesbian Task Force (www.thetaskforce.org) can provide you with a listing of state and local community centers, along with a wealth of other resources and political action alerts.

6

....

Take Care

LGBT people aren't alone in being subjected to discrimination—people of color, women, and the poor, among others, have also been long-standing targets of social injustice. The receiving end of institutional and interpersonal prejudice is a dangerous place for anyone to be. And sometimes the hurt from outside makes us strike inward instead of fighting back. Perhaps the most insidious impact of discrimination is when it causes us to absorb the negative messages unconsciously—and to give up on ourselves because we start believing that we don't deserve the physical, emotional, or spiritual well-being that is every person's innate right.

Our opponents understand that attacking our self-esteem is one of their most powerful weapons. If vast numbers of us don't think we're worthy of equality, they'll win without a fight, at the expense of our safety and well-being. In this section, our contributors entreat us all to take care of ourselves and each other. They believe we're all worth it, and they're right.

—*Angela Watrous*

Stop Hate Before It Kills

Judy Shepard, Founder and Executive Director,
Matthew Shepard Foundation

In October 1998, my precious son Matthew, who happened to be gay, was murdered. The incident prompted unprecedented media coverage and focused the nation's attention on anti-gay hate crimes.

Prior to Matt's death, I was a wife and mother, leading a fairly sheltered life. I quickly learned that my son's violent death was actually a common occurrence if you were a member, or perceived to be a member, of the LGBT community. This knowledge prompted my family to create a foundation in Matthew's memory to encourage acceptance and embrace diversity.

Since Matthew's death, I have been traveling the nation and trying to stem the tide of hate that is eating away at our culture. I speak at schools, churches, corporations; I speak to anyone who is willing to take a moment to listen.

It's clear that in some ways our nation has become a more accepting place. However, there has been scant progress in other areas, particularly in terms of legislation that secures rights and basic protections for the gay community. It sometimes feels to me as if we are living in a nation at odds with itself—an America that tunes in to be entertained by popular, gay-themed TV programming but turns a blind eye to the injustices LGBT people still face.

In 2003, more than 30 American cities and towns reported hate crimes against gays. The vast majority of such crimes do not garner national head-lines like my son's murder did: Sakia Gunn, a 15-year-old lesbian, was fatally stabbed in Newark, New Jersey; F.C. Martinez, a transgender 16-year-old Navajo, was murdered in a hate-motivated attack in Cortez, Colorado; Gwen Araujo, a 17-year-old Latina transgender youth, was killed in Newark, California. The list goes on and on.

We must all work together to find grassroots solutions to this problem of gay hatred and prejudice against all minorities. I believe that bigotry is rooted in ignorance, a lack of knowledge, about minorities. That ignorance can only be overcome with the coming-out process—not only for LGBT people but for family and friends as well. It is necessary for family and friends of all minorities to come out and talk about what our loved ones are experiencing.

We also have the opportunity as parents to teach our children to understand and accept diversity long before hate can provoke violent reactions to gay issues. Ten percent of all hate crimes occur at schools and colleges. A gay teen is bashed; a disabled teen is tormented; a Jewish, African American, or Muslim teen is taunted. The cycle just continues, until that hate-filled child becomes a citizen in our community and, sometimes, a perpetrator. We must "arm" children with an education in tolerance before their formative school years begin, and then require our educators to continue the job. Hate is a learned behavior, but it's never too late to empower a young adult with the tools to improve his or her life choices, to embrace acceptance and a belief in equality.

The consequences of hate hurt everyone: victims, perpetrators, and all of their families. Lives are ended, and lives are changed forever. If a change is to be made, let's make it a positive one.

⋛ STEPS FOR EQUALITY ⋚

+ Report all hate crimes. This will allow local crime to became part of the national crime statistics kept by the FBI, giving us a far more accurate picture of the level of violence directed against the LGBT community.

+ Teach children to accept and understand diversity.

+ Support organizations, such as the Matthew Shepard Foundation (www.matthewshepard.org), that work to prevent hate crimes through education, as well as organizations that help the victims of hate crimes and their families.

Unite against Violence

Tina D'Elia and Andy Wong, Staff Members,
Community United Against Violence

From hate crimes to partner abuse, violence or the threat of violence greatly impacts LGBT people. It can keep us from coming out and engaging in healthy, fulfilling relationships. It can make us afraid to hold hands with our partners while strolling down the street. It can destroy the sanctity of our homes. And, in the most extreme cases, it can take our lives or the lives of those we love. Only by uniting against violence toward LGBT people—and by taking action against all forms of oppression, including racism, sexism, homophobia, ableism, classism, and ageism—can we achieve true equality.

The first place we should always be safe is at home. The intense societal scrutiny under which LGBT relationships operate makes it hard for us to admit that domestic violence impacts some of us. Both the LGBT community and members of abusive couples fear that evidence of trouble in our relationships will provide our adversaries with ammunition to use against our relationships and our families. The entrenched idea that only men are abusers also contributes to a lack of awareness of domestic violence in lesbian relationships, and many people incorrectly assume that gay men's domestic violence is a fight between equals, and thus a victimless situation. In truth, as LGBT people fall in love or lust, we can also fall victim to the same unhealthy dynamics of power and control that lead to violence in straight relationships. Speaking out about domestic violence and seeking LGBT-friendly counseling is the path to strength and healing.

Our understanding of hate violence—and how that violence impacts LGBT people—has evolved over the decades. While strangers attacking us on the street or other public places still make up the largest portion of incidents reported, we now know that anti-LGBT hate incidents occur in schools, workplaces, prisons, and home settings—and that perpetrators are sometimes loved ones, known community members, or members of the police force. At Community United Against Violence (CUAV), we receive more than a thousand calls each year from courageous survivors seeking emergency help. We offer them free counseling, legal advocacy, and emergency aid. Since statistics show that most gay bashers are likely to be under the age of 21 and that people who know a LGBT person are less likely to become bashers, we also have a local Speakers Bureau that visits elementary, middle, and high schools to help forge connections between LGBT people and children and teens.

As the LGBT community becomes more visible and vocal, we can also become targets of those who are vehemently, even violently opposed to change. Only together, with the help of our straight allies, can we cope with and work to prevent the violence around us.

⇒ STEPS FOR EQUALITY ⇐

+ Recognize that all forms of physical, emotional, and verbal abuse are destructive and unacceptable. To learn the signs, go to www.gmdvp.org or www.avp.org.

+ Volunteer for an LGBT anti-violence organization. At CUAV, we offer opportunities to counsel individuals through our crisis line or to speak out to young people in classrooms. For information on the nearest anti-violence group in your area, check out NCAVP's website at www.ncavp.org.

+ Organize or participate in an event that celebrates the survival, healing, and empowerment of former victims of violence and mourns those that have been lost. Take Back the Night rallies and vigils are a great example of how to host such events (www.takebackthenight.org).

+ If you're in a position to help an LGBT person affected by violence, listen, believe, and ask how you can be helpful in her recovery. Suggest resources rather than telling someone what to do, trying to rescue him, or speaking judgmentally. Offer to help in realistic ways and accept that hate and domestic violence take time to heal. Telling someone to put it behind her can be harmful if the person is not ready to move on.

Demand Equality in Health Care

Joel Ginsberg, Executive Director, Gay and Lesbian Medical Association

A closeted lesbian goes to see her doctor. The doctor asks the patient if she is sexually active. When she replies that she is, the doctor asks what she is using for birth control. The patient becomes uncomfortable and mumbles something about condoms. In the future, she avoids going to see the doctor and misses opportunities to be screened for breast cancer, gynecological cancers, and other health issues.

A man who has sex with men is assumed to be heterosexual by his health care provider. The provider therefore does not recommend that the patient receive a vaccination against hepatitis A, a serious and easily transmissible—but completely preventable—disease that is more common among gay and bisexual men than in the general population. The man later becomes ill with hepatitis.

A transgender person goes to see a health care provider for routine care. The provider feels uncomfortable, so he says he lacks sufficient knowledge to treat the patient, even though the patient's ailment has nothing to do with gender.

In each of these examples we see that homophobia and transphobia—fear and ignorance related to sexual orientation and gender identity—can be hazardous to one's health. To get good health care, each of us must have a provider we can be honest with about our sexual behavior and gender identity, and our providers must be knowledgeable about our unique health concerns.

Most people know that men who have sex with men are at increased risk of contracting HIV/AIDS if they practice unsafe sex. Many people do not realize, however, that because of the emotional impact of homophobia and transphobia, LGBT people are more likely than others to abuse alcohol, tobacco, and other substances and are at increased risk for depression and anxiety. And, though it's not widely acknowledged, domestic violence does occur in same-sex relationships.

To stay healthy, LGBT people need to find compassionate and knowledgeable providers and then ask questions pertinent to their health. In particular, men who have sex with men should talk to their health care providers about prevention of or treatment for HIV/AIDS and other sexually transmitted diseases (STDs), depression, hepatitis immunization, genital warts and anal cancer, and smoking-related illnesses. Women who have sex with women are not immune from STDs and should ask how to prevent them. Women should also talk to their health care providers about breast, lung, and gynecological cancers; depression; and cardiovascular health. (Among lesbians, lower rates of childbearing, oral contraceptive use, and cancer screenings—as well as higher rates of obesity, smoking, and alcohol abuse—are risk factors for cancer and heart disease.)

Transgender people face many barriers to achieving health and safety, in no small part because of hate-motivated violence and discrimination in housing and employment. Denial of care and medical mistreatment are common, as is the refusal of health insurers to provide coverage for essential hormones and surgeries. For transgender people, it's critical to find a health care provider who is welcoming and knowledgeable about trans needs.

> ⋝ **STEPS FOR EQUALITY** ⋜

+ Find an LGBT-friendly health care provider at www.glma.org.

+ Refer your provider to www.glma.org for guidelines in treating LGBT patients.

+ Ask your employer to provide health insurance for domestic partners (you can find a helpful manual entitled *How to Achieve Domestic Partner Benefits in the Workplace* at www.hrc.org).

+ Find out how you can take action in your community by signing up for GLMA's email alerts at www.glma.org.

Stay Sane in a Crazy World

Kimeron Hardin, Psychologist and Author

Despite the fact that millions of Americans see some type of mental health professional each year, most choose to hide it. No matter how many celebrities admit in the tabloids that they struggle with depression, panic, or addiction, the stigma associated with mental illness is still pervasive. In addition to this stigma, queer people must contend with a homophobic culture in which many believe sexual orientation is a mental illness or a sin. No wonder some queer people avoid acknowledging that they are struggling emotionally: in some cases, admitting that you need help can feel like you're validating the ignorant stereotypes that you've fought so hard to resist.

As someone who grew up gay in the South during the '60s, I well understand these fears. No one I knew talked about family secrets or sought the advice of psychotherapists, despite the Tennessee Williams plots many of us were living. It took a slew of undergraduate and graduate psychology courses, my own personal journey through depression, and good psychotherapy for me to finally understand that depression was rampant in my family, and that talking about it was a good thing.

Depression and anxiety are equal opportunity afflictions. They can affect anyone—rich or poor, old or young, black or white, gay or straight. Depression is so ubiquitous that one out of every ten Americans will experience at least one episode of depression this year, and approximately 80 percent improve with treatment.[1] Unfortunately, nearly two-thirds of people affected by a mental illness do not seek treatment.[2]

Being lesbian, gay, bisexual, or transgender doesn't cause depression or anxiety, though it does present unique cultural and social challenges that can contribute to existing emotional difficulties. When we grow up hearing from our families, our schools, our religious institutions, and our media that being queer is a bad thing, it can lead us to hide a big part of ourselves to try to fit in. We learn to invalidate our feelings or desires and pack them into a secret self, as a form of emotional and physical protection, which can then make it difficult later to find and experience true intimacy with our partner.

It's hard not to internalize the homophobic and heterosexist comments we hear all around us every day. And when we absorb the cultural message that we are second-class citizens, we miss promising opportunities, or, in extreme cases, we make self-destructive choices.

Despite homophobic cultural messages, the lack of full family recognition, the disparaging attitudes of our major religious institutions and our current president, mental illness is not the norm within the LGBT community. Still, if you suffer from a mental illness, muster the courage to seek the help you need. If you feel you don't have a classic depression or anxiety disorder, but you still have old scars that could use some healing clear the way for better relationships, more productivity, and greater life satisfaction, *reach out for support*. It's a sign of strength and courage—not an admission that your sexuality is the problem.

⋛ STEPS FOR EQUALITY ⋚

+ Never participate in so-called reparative therapy, or psychotherapy designed to "convert" an LGBT person to heterosexuality. These types of treatments, opposed by every major mental health organization, not only have been shown to be ineffective, but they actually lead to increased depression, anxiety, and self-destructiveness.[3]

+ Make a commitment to take better care of yourself and those relationships in your life that are important to you. Nurturing goes both ways.

+ Recognize that admitting you are depressed, anxious, trapped in unhealthy patterns, or emotionally overwhelmed does not mean that you are weak or flawed. Taking steps to get help is actually a sign of strength and can lead to greater life satisfaction.

+ Look for LGBT-identified or LGBT-affirmative mental health professionals or ask specifically to be referred to a lesbian or gay therapist through your insurance company (see Resources).

- Find a support group in your area that offers you a place to be yourself and express your feelings without judgment. Check with your local mental health center or the nearest LGBT community center (see Resources).

- Access additional help through self-help books written for LGBT people and their loved ones (see Resources).

Take the Blame out of AIDS

Craig E. Thompson, Executive Director, AIDS Project Los Angeles

One of my old photographs shows a dozen gay men celebrating my 30th birthday on Fire Island. It was a happy occasion, yet if you look closely you can see that some of the young faces and bodies bear the encroaching signs of AIDS. There are just four of us left of that dozen.

A few years after that photograph was taken, I moved from New York to Los Angeles with my partner for work and a change of scenery, and to occupy my time before I died. This was the calculus of the time. For reasons I can't ever know, I have survived while so many others died, and for more than a decade I have worked in HIV/AIDS. Mine is a common story— far from unique—about what it has meant to be gay in the age of AIDS.

We could not have foreseen then that AIDS would become the greatest economic, political, and social struggle of our time. We could not have known that our personal, inexplicable losses would multiply into 20 million deaths of AIDS globally. What becomes clear as AIDS explodes around the world is that our experience as a community is not lodged in the past, but is a very present reminder of how, in the absence of leadership, average citizens can mobilize for life. And life, with its many blessings and brutalities, is what we seek.

During the height of the AIDS epidemic, all over this country gay men and lesbians, and the people who loved us, joined together out of panic and emerged as warriors. This country was shaken to its very foundations by the vigor, candor, and craft we brought to the task of putting a face on AIDS and demanding that attention be paid. We wrote the playbook on mobilization. We must now translate it into the world's many languages and place it in the hands of those who fight AIDS across the globe.

Some have argued that AIDS careened directly into the path of gay sexual liberation, which was making its steady progression from pathology to an increasing celebration of healthy sexual expression. AIDS has always been located at the intersection of politics and public health. And now AIDS seems more marginalized than ever, despite rising infection rates in minority communities and among gay men. To talk about AIDS is to talk about sex and drug use, and increasingly, the plight of the poor and communities of color. It has never been easy to talk about AIDS, but silence still equals death.

We live in a world where, by and large, it still goes against societal norms to be gay, or "other," or sick, or in need of help. This may be why we have spent 23 years assigning blame for the spread of HIV/AIDS; we have blamed people (white gay men, addicts, single mothers, and black men on the down low), behaviors (bare-backing and crystal use), and even venues (bathhouses and prisons).

Blame is the enemy of pride. As we celebrate our gay pride every June— and every day—we cannot forget that with pride comes a host of other benefits: health, happiness, prosperity. Supporting people with HIV/AIDS and the organizations that serve them is an act of community pride that heals ruptures and advances equality.

Blame is also a failure of imagination, without which we will never bring an end to AIDS. If the LGBT community and our allies cannot imagine a future without AIDS, no one can.

⇒ STEPS FOR EQUALITY ⇐

+ Act locally. Organizations that work with people living with, or at risk for, HIV/AIDS need your time, your experience, and your wisdom. Connect, or reconnect, with an AIDS organization near you and give freely of your time and energy. Visit www.thebody.com/hotlines/other.html for a state-by-state list of HIV/AIDS organizations.

+ Live by example. Remember the power that resides in each of us to influence the decisions of our partners, our friends, our family, and our communities. Take pride in leading a safe, sober, and productive life.

Advocate for Our Elders

Scott J. Hamilton, Deputy Executive Director, Services and
Advocacy for GLBT Elders (SAGE)

Marion and Catherine, old friends of mine, moved from Canada to New York together 48 years ago. They attended nursing school together, worked together, and lived together all of that time. They were never really thought of as lesbians by others, just as "the girls." Labels aside, this couple shared a deep love and commitment to each other. They built a life of joy, adventure, and companionship that saw each of them through difficult times. Catherine and Marion were committed to being together forever.

But forever ended last summer. A little over a year after Catherine was diagnosed with Alzheimer's, she left the home she shared with Marion and returned to Canada to live with her sister. Since Marion and Catherine were "just friends," Catherine's family believed they had the right and responsibility to make decisions regarding her health and her future.

Now Marion is lonely and desperately misses her partner. She worries that she will be alone for the rest of her life. Since she was never really out, her friends can't understand the depth of her loss and aren't aware of how difficult this situation is for Marion. She didn't come out as a young woman because of fear. And she can't come out now for the same reason. So Marion suffers largely in silence, isolated from friends, family, and community.

Carl, another friend of mine, lives not far from Marion. He retired from an investment bank a couple of years ago. He was, by any standards, extremely successful in his career. He serves as a trustee for his alma mater and is generous with his time and money. But Carl's accomplishments, great as they are, simply couldn't fill a void that existed in his life. So Carl took advantage of the life changes inherent in retirement and began the process of coming out.

No longer tethered to a conservative work environment, Carl eased his way into the LGBT community. First he ventured into a gay bar. Then Carl sought out a book discussion group comprised largely of other retired gay men. Soon Carl assembled a group of new friends and is now dating one of those friends.

Marion and Carl don't live in different cities. In fact, they even share a zip code. But their experiences are indicative of the myriad challenges and opportunities that we face as LGBT people. As I consider my own aging future, I do so with a mixture of apprehension, satisfaction, hope, and gratitude.

Gratitude may seem a little odd, but not long ago everybody figured there wouldn't be many gay men who lived long enough to get old. As I continue the march toward my later years, I do so grateful that there are a lot of us on similar journeys. In fact, by 2020 there will more than 6 million LGBT people at or near retirement age; a full 25 percent of our community will be over 50 years old. And that's reason for gratitude.

We have unique concerns and needs, and those will continue to grow as our community ages. But LGBT folks have come together around so many issues that I believe we can come together around aging too. We have to rethink aging and all of the possibilities it holds. We must advocate for our Marions and welcome our Carls with open hearts. We need to celebrate the old among us and look forward to our own later years. We have to *be* community for all the members of our community. And, lucky for us, that's something already we know a little about.

⇒ STEPS FOR EQUALITY ⇐

+ Examine your own prejudices concerning aging, and dedicate some time to supporting older LGBT people in your life or in your community. Older LGBT people often have fewer financial and social resources than heterosexual elders, which means that younger members of the LGBT community must rally around our elders and offer friendship and support (see Resources).

+ Create a safe, welcoming environment—in your home, place of worship, community center—where older LGBT people can celebrate their lives and be themselves.

+ Make financial and social preparations now that will help guarantee your full enjoyment of your later years.

Keep the Faith

Reverend Dr. Troy D. Perry, Founder, Metropolitan Community Churches

In 1968, I was going through a rough time. I had been rejected by my former church when the church members discovered I was gay. I experienced a failed relationship. I got depressed, lost my perspective, and hit bottom. I attempted suicide.

In the midst of my despair, I began to listen to what many faith communities call the "still, small voice of God." I began to believe that God created LGBT people just as we are—and that God loves us just as we are. I began to believe that there could be a church for LGBT people who had experienced rejection in other faith communities.

In the process of reconciling my sexuality and my spirituality, I discovered an important truth: God's followers aren't necessarily on the same wavelength with God. Too many religions have allowed human-based traditions to creep into their beliefs. Others have adopted society's biases. And some religious leaders have exercised their own control issues and imposed their internal emotional problems on their religious followers.

When the Spirit moves you, you should first listen, and then you must act. In my faith tradition, we call it "taking a step of faith." So I listened to God's Spirit—and then I took a step of faith. I put an ad in a local paper announcing that I was starting a church in which LGBT people could grow in their faith and explore their spirituality. On that first Sunday, 12 people showed up to worship at my home in Huntington Park, California. That group grew into the first Metropolitan Community Church (MCC), and within two years it had attracted a congregation of more than 1,000 predominantly LGBT people. Today, there are MCC churches in 23 countries, and each year more than 225,000 people attend services and programs.

Increasingly LGBT people are reclaiming our spirituality. No one else can define us or limit us. We've reclaimed the positive, hope-filled message of our faith, and worked to liberate it from the biases and prejudices that too many religious leaders imposed on it. We've created our own positive, creative places of worship.

Over the last two decades, the LGBT spirituality movement has blossomed. Today, there are predominantly LGBT temples for Jews, and LGBT faith groups for Muslims. Every major religious denomination in Christianity has an LGBT-affirming group that is working for spiritual change from within.

Here's what I believe with all my heart: LGBT people are created by God as physical beings, emotional beings, and intellectual beings, but we're also created as *spiritual* beings. No individual or group has the right to deny us the Creator's love and blessing in our lives. Through spiritual faith, we can all discover new depths to love, hope, forgiveness, wholeness, and fulfillment in life.

≥ STEPS FOR EQUALITY ≤

+ Make time in your life each day to listen to the "still, small voice" of the Creator. When the Spirit moves you, take a step of faith, and discover that God really loves you, just as you are.

+ Learn more about LGBT spiritual groups by reading books or visiting websites (see Resources).

+ Visit www.truluck.com for excellent resources that can help LGBT people reclaim the positive message of the Bible, and for biblical interpretations that are free of anti-LGBT biases.

+ Learn more about LGBT-friendly interpretations of the Bible at the Center for Lesbian and Gay Studies in Religion and Ministry (www.clgs.org) and at the Metropolitan Community Church of San Francisco (www.mccsf.org).

+ Visit one of the many faith groups where you can be open about both your spirituality and your sexuality (see Resources).

+ Believe in yourself and your faith. Don't let any person or group deny your right to spirituality.

+ Straight allies can encourage their own houses of worship to become "open and affirming" of the LGBT community. Excellent resources are available from the United Church of Christ and can be adapted by other faith communities. To learn more, visit www.ucccoalition.org.

Make the World Safe for LGBT People

William F. Schulz, Executive Director, Amnesty International

After finishing his university degree, Wissam, a 27-year-old Lebanese man, took a job in Cairo as a web programmer and database designer. One day another foreign man contacted him on a gay website. "I've just arrived here," the man wrote, "and I don't know anybody. Could you introduce me to Cairo and the community?"

Wissam agreed, and the two met at a café for coffee. But no sooner had they sat down than four burly men approached, grabbed Wissam—literally lifting him off the ground—and stuffed him in a police car. So began an odyssey that was to result in over a year's imprisonment for the crime of "debauchery." Wissam's private conversations with the man over the Internet were used as evidence against him.

Over the past few years, nearly 200 men have been arrested in Egypt because of their sexual orientation. In Jamaica, lesbians and gay men have been beaten and raped on account of their sexuality. Famous reggae performers have encouraged the shooting, stoning, and drowning of gay people in the lyrics of their songs. And in Honduras, dozens of transgender people and gay men have been murdered by their fellow citizens, including by the police.

While enormous progress has been made in the struggle for civil rights for LGBT people—particularly in Canada, Western Europe, and even, despite recent setbacks, the United States—some 70 countries still criminalize homosexual relationships between consenting adults, with penalties ranging from fines to torture to death.

Fortunately, during the past 15 years, defenders of LGBT rights have emerged in virtually every corner of the globe. In Jamaica, for example, J-FLAG, the major lesbian and gay organization in that country, has become a powerful voice of protest and protection. But the international community must play a critical role in reinforcing these kinds of national efforts. We must frame the struggle for rights in global terms and fight for justice for every LGBT person.

In the spring of 2004, the United Nations Commission on Human Rights introduced a landmark resolution calling for the protection of all people—including lesbians and gay men—from human rights abuses. But, thanks in part to the United States—the only Western government that failed to support the measure—this resolution never came to a final vote. Although resolutions adopted by the UN Commission on Human Rights do not include enforcement mechanisms, they do help establish human rights norms and they can be used to pressure governments, including our own, to revise their legal codes and conform their practices to international standards. And that's why the groundbreaking resolution must be reintroduced.

The struggle for full and equal rights around the world will be a long one, but ultimately the arc of the universe always bends toward justice. In the meantime, it's our job to grab onto the arc and give it a pull.

⋝ STEPS FOR EQUALITY ⋜

+ Contact the Secretary of State to demand that a similar UN Human Rights Commission resolution be introduced in 2005, with backing from the United States. Send your letters to: The Secretary of State, U.S. Department of State, 2201 C Street, NW, Washington, DC 20520; go to http://contact-us.state.gov and click on "Send a message to the Secretary of State"; or call 202-647-4000.

+ Join Amnesty International USA's OUTfront Network (www.amnesty usa.org/outfront) to organize with others on behalf of LGBT human rights causes, contact government representatives both in the United States and abroad about critical LGBT human rights cases, and send messages of support and solidarity to LGBT individuals in prison or under threat for their lifestyles or their political activities.

+ Support local LGBT organizations, especially in developing countries where activists are often working under difficult circumstances without

---

easy access to resources. For such organizations, even a small contribution can make an enormous difference. One such organization is J-FLAG in Jamaica (www.jflag.org). OUTfront (www.amnestyusa.org/outfront) can offer additional suggestions.

section

7

....

Create an Equal
Society

Big change requires visionary ideas accompanied by brave action. In this section, contributors think big: they tell us how we can take our activism beyond the limitations of our own lives, homes, relationships, and law books—and into everyday society. They speak to the importance of viewing TV and other media with equality-colored glasses, of bringing LGBT issues into the workplace and the workout place, and of creating safe spaces where we can let our hair down and rejuvenate. They understand that change needs to take place throughout society in order for us to achieve equality. And they encourage us to bring about that change by engaging with the communities where we live and work, rather than reflexively exiling ourselves from them. As utterly fabulous as we are, we owe it to the world to share ourselves. If we do, we—along with our ever-growing ranks of supporters—will prevail in creating a more just society, and a world in which we'd all prefer to live.

—Angela Watrous

Liberate Yourself from Labels: Bisexuality and Beyond

Rebecca Walker, Author and Activist

People who love both genders are the subject of all kinds of misguided stereotypes: that all bisexual people are promiscuous, that we're incapable of monogamy, that we're not "really" gay or "really" straight. The truth is, the only difference between bi people and others is that we have the flexibility—whether by choice or design—to be sexual with both genders. We're a diverse group of people, just like any other segment of the population, and we deserve to be recognized for who we are as individuals.

Instead of asking what gay and straight people should understand about being bisexual, I think we need to ask what gay, straight, bisexual, and transgender people need to understand about permanent liberation from divisive thought itself. I would much rather work on dismantling the mental boundaries we have created in a misguided attempt to avert the truth of our interconnectedness. Homophobia and heterophobia are only the symptoms of the problem. Let's get to the root. Can you stop your mind from slicing the world into tiny, seemingly irreconcilable pieces? Can I?

Bisexual people need what everyone else needs: food, air, clear water. Freedom from persecution and the threat of annihilation. A reasonable way to make a living. As long as we're not hurting anyone, it would be nice to be able to move freely without having to explain ourselves and our choices. It would be nice to be free of both the heavy pronouncements of religious morality and the earnest judgmentalism of politically correct progressives.

This business of convincing each other, group by group, of our right to exist is taking so long, I'm not sure it's working. Our survival as a species may depend on our ability to change the way we see the world right now. Straight, gay, bisexual, transgender —what does it matter? Have you found ways to minimize territoriality, labeling, anger, jealousy in your own life? Have you found ways to address your own assumptions and judgments? These are the questions we must all pursue if we're ever going to join together as happy, confident, and integrated human beings.

⋛ STEPS FOR EQUALITY ⋚

+ Avoid making judgments about people based on generalizations and stereotypes. While you're at it, avoid making judgments about people at all. Make up your mind about people based on your actual experiences with them.

+ Try to let go of "us and them" thinking. We're all sexual beings, and this similarity is a much greater truth than any differences our culture has manufactured.

+ Don't assume you know about someone's sexuality based on appearances or what you think you know about bisexual people. A man dating a woman may be bisexual; a woman married to another woman may be bisexual. In the same way that heterosexual married couples still experience attraction to other members of the opposite sex, a bisexual person maintains his or her sexual identity even while in a monogamous relationship. Being in a committed relationship doesn't change our sexuality; it just brings our various expressions of sexuality into a tighter focus.

Fuel Your Activism with Pride

Reverend Dr. D. Mark Wilson, Assistant Professor,
The Pacific School of Religion

Thee rivers of identity flow into my one brown body and swell my pride as an African American gay man: my black history and heritage; my Christian faith; and my own body, awash in same-sex love, desire, affection, and attraction. Building on the words of my friend and mentor, Rev. Dr. Jeremiah Wright, I've come to describe myself as unashamedly black, unapologetically Christian, and proudly gay. I take great pride in all of these aspects of my identity.

While these three parts of myself are inseparable, it's not uncommon for others to perceive them as inherently in conflict. When I came out one Sunday morning to my rather conservative black Baptist church, where I serve as pastor, one Sunday morning, I put the Christian love professed by my members to the test. Some of them went on the attack, writing hate mail, distributing flyers throughout the neighborhood in an attempt to ruin my ministry and reputation, and calling a church meeting to vote me out. But my pride fueled me as I continued to preach the same love that had transformed my own internalized homophobia and self-hate as a gay teen, in hopes that it could also transform these members of my congregation. After five months of major church conflict, the majority of my congregation—both those who'd supported me from the start and those who hadn't—voted to love and affirm me as their pastor. The voice of a gay Baptist preacher would be heard in our African American church.

Though I was fueled with pride, this experience was painful and difficult, but not so different from coming out as a person of faith among friends in the gay and lesbian political community, who still find it strange and unbelievable that my black Baptist congregation loved and affirmed me. And on some level, I understood my friends' confusion. In the growing conservatism of the last presidential election, hate-mongers and religious extremists in the Christian faith did everything in their power to destroy the rights and gains of both racial minorities and of gay and lesbian people seeking equal marital rights. Twenty black clergy in my hometown of Oakland, California, supported a presidential candidate with whom they disagreed on most issues solely because of his crusade against same-sex marriage.

Though I have found much love and support among African American congregations, how distant and alien I sometimes feel among my own. This alienation seems similar to the racism I have experienced among white gay men and lesbians, including the men at a gay resort in Puerto Vallarta who thought it would be humorous to say to me, "No niggers into the pool" and "Don't be doing those nigger dances in here."

On the cultural margins between the African American and LGBT communities, I encounter both the homophobia driven by religion and the racism perpetuated by those who know all too well what it means to be hated and left out. In the most challenging and most triumphant moments, it's my pride that I draw upon: my pride as a Christian encourages me to preach prophetic words of justice and inclusive love; my pride as an African American sways me to call on ancient grandmother spirits to sing the songs that bring the walls of difference tumbling down; and my pride as a same-gender loving man keeps my feet dancing, even in the face of hate, to the rhythm of "I Will Survive."

> ⋛ **STEPS FOR EQUALITY** ⋚

+ Honor the many voices, languages, styles, songs, dances, and cultures that make up our collective identity and spirit.

+ Take pride in all of who you are, and don't let anyone suggest that the different parts of yourself don't belong together. For me, that's meant honoring the faith that has taught me, the African American heritage that has brought me here, and the God-given pleasures and attractions that make my body and loving real.

Get the Scoop on Creating A Gay-Friendly Workplace

Jerry Greenfield, Cofounder, Ben & Jerry's Homemade

When Ben and I opened our first Scoop Shop in 1978 in an old Burlington, Vermont, gas station, we were two big guys with one big idea: we wanted to make the best ice cream in the world, and we wanted to have fun doing it. The only benefit we could offer our coworkers in those days was the Employee Smoking Lounge: a couple of milk crates out by the dumpster.

Much to our surprise, the company grew. Noting that, we got another big idea: to use our business as a force for good in the world. We figured the best place to start was right at home, by treating our employees the way we'd want to be treated and creating the kind of workplace where we'd enjoy working. When we built our first manufacturing plant in 1984, we were able to start offering our employees a few things that were even cooler than the smoking lounge. We set up a lactation room where moms could breastfeed their babies. We opened a nap room where people could catch a few Zs. And in 1989, when we finally found an insurance company that would let us do it, we started offering domestic partner benefits to our lesbian and gay employees, and to the unmarried straight folks too. Now all our benefits are for all our employees: family leave, counseling, and (our favorite new benefit) reimbursement for buying a hybrid car.

We've always had a lot of gay people at Ben & Jerry's. Why, you ask? Well, for starters, when we began the company, I was coaching a women's softball team, so that gave us a pretty good connection to the extensive lesbian community in Burlington, Vermont. Another factor was that, being oddball guys ourselves, we had nothing against hiring non-mainstream people. In fact, we preferred it. We were trying to set a tone and create an atmosphere of acceptance in the company. Also, we liked hiring people who shared our values, who saw the world the way we did, and who appreciated the differences between people. In short, we wanted people in our company who believed in what we believed in. Not surprisingly, that made Ben & Jerry's attractive to employees—including LGBT people—who didn't want to be discriminated against and didn't want to have any part in discriminating against anyone else. Pretty simple, really.

⋛ STEPS FOR EQUALITY ⋚

If you're an employer or supervisor:

+ Offer diversity training to employees at all levels.

+ Establish a company policy that values diversity and explicitly addresses the repercussions for intolerance or harassment. Make sure to offer equal personal, partner, and family benefits to LGBT employees. To learn more about how to become an equal opportunity employer, go to the Social Venture Network's website (www.svn.org).

+ Treat your employees as you'd want to be treated.

+ In your public relations and recruitment campaigns, promote your commitment to being an equality-minded employer. This will help other employers see the wisdom in this strategy.

If you're an employee:

+ Treat your colleagues as you want to be treated. Be respectful of differences; value each other's opinions and experiences. If appropriate, ask about each other's families, and treat everyone's families with the same interest.

+ Express to your employer that you appreciate their support of LGBT employees, regardless of your own sexual orientation. Make suggestions for how your workplace could be more queer-friendly, whether you do so at stockholder's meetings, at the water cooler, or in an email to your supervisor. Go to www.svn.org for more information on how to support equality in your workplace.

Keep a Queer Eye on the Media

Joan M. Garry, former Executive Director,
Gay & Lesbian Alliance Against Defamation (GLAAD)

Whenever I'm confronted with news of another hate crime or another hate law, I take some comfort in remembering that homophobia is not a natural human state. Babies are not born hating anyone. And because people are taught to be homophobic, they can be taught otherwise.

As activists for equality, there are many ways we can help move our society toward understanding and accepting LGBT people. We can work to change our government, our communities, and even ourselves. We must also keep an eye on the media—one of the greatest cultural influences in our society—to make sure that we challenge and prevent homophobic images, whether they are created by ignorance or by malice. Most important, LGBT people and our straight allies must be visible in all our diversity. The anti-gay right wants nothing more than to make us invisible. And our visibility is what is winning the long term—in the 2004 election exit polls, 64 percent of American voters said they believe that same-sex relationships should receive some form of legal recognition.

The media is one of our greatest hopes for addressing homophobic attitudes and perceptions, so we must ensure that the words and images put forth by the media are part of the solution and not part of the problem. If it seems daunting to try to change the bent of news coverage and entertainment in this country, just think back to a time when the words "gay" and "lesbian" were taboo in the media. It wasn't until after a 1987 meeting with GLAAD, for example, that the *New York Times* changed its editorial policy and began using the word "gay." Fifteen years later, GLAAD's Announcing Equality Project has led more than 500 newspapers across the country—including the *New York Times*—to publish same-sex union announcements alongside other wedding listings.

Still, more change is needed. We have to continue to hold media professionals—journalists, directors, producers, writers, actors, musicians, and executives—accountable for the way they tell the stories of LGBT people. When we see something that depicts LGBT people in an unfair or sensationalistic manner, we take action, sometimes with behind-the-scenes conversations and sometimes with very public campaigns. What makes our pressure work is *your* willingness to pick up the phone, write a letter, send an email, make a donation, and, if necessary, boycott a product.

Besides responding to defamation, we also ask for more of what we'd like to see: more fair, accurate, and inclusive representations of LGBT people in newspapers, movies, radio, and TV. When you see examples of the media getting things right, you can reward those representations with your attention, praise, and your consumer dollars. For instance, you might consider attending the annual GLAAD Media Awards to celebrate the year's successes and to thank media producers for their progress on issues important to the LGBT community.

The national debate about gay and lesbian families, regarding our right to exist and our right to be treated fairly, will not end—nor will our voices diminish—until we win. We will achieve full equality in this country, including the right to marry, but our visibility is the key to victory. The media plays a vital role in amplifying our visibility, our humanity, and our stories, which are already causing a revolution in the world's understanding and acceptance of our lives.

≥ STEPS FOR EQUALITY ≤

+ Watch, read, listen, and surf media carefully, knowing that it's not just a one-way communication. Sign up for email action alerts at www.glaad.org.

+ Use media to amplify your own personal acts of visibility. Sign up for a media training with GLAAD to learn how to get local media to cover your events and how to become a spokesperson for your community.

+ Announce the celebration of a same-sex union—whether your own or your loved one's—in one of the U.S. newspapers that print such announcements.

+ Write letters to the editor in which you identify yourself with pride.

Come Out of the
Locker Room Closet

Dan Woog, Author and Soccer Coach

A t the end of a high school soccer match, it's traditional for both teams to line up and shake hands. One day, after the team I coach beat our archrivals, I heard an opponent tell our player, "Nice game, faggot."

"No, I'm pretty sure he likes girls," I quickly said. "I'm the one who likes guys."

Only a few of my athletes heard the remark, but they laughed—with me, and at him. The opposing player, though, was mystified. He'd lost the game, tried a typical teenage taunt, and found he was mocked instead. He had plenty to process on the ride home.

That's just one of many positive experiences I've had as an openly gay high school soccer coach. For years I was afraid to come out. I feared losing the respect of my players, the support of their parents, even my job.

But when I came out, none of that happened. In fact, the reaction was just the opposite. People applauded my "courage." Athletes remarked on my "honesty." And the wall that I'd imagined was separating me from my teammates vanished.

No player has ever come out to me while I've coached him (though after graduation, several have). But because I've been open about my life, players now talk with me about aspects of their lives—an alcoholic mother, an out-of-work father, even girlfriend problems—that they did not feel comfortable sharing with me before. Talking things out takes pressure off them. They concentrate more, play better—and that's a winning situation for all of us.

When I came out, I imagined it would be a one-time event. I didn't realize that each year I'd coach a new crop of freshmen. Every fall, one of the newcomers makes an anti-gay crack. But I don't say anything. Without fail—or prompting from me—an upperclassman scurries over and talks to the ninth grader. The younger player's eyes grow wide—but he also gets the message: Don't say homophobic stuff. It's not cool.

I can't overemphasize how important it is for me to be out with my athletes—and to be out with humor. For example, one day someone spray-painted "Robbie is very gay" near our bench. The players gathered that afternoon, saw the graffiti, and apprehensively awaited my reaction.

"Wow," I said. "Somebody really misspelled my first name."

They laughed, and practice began.

The next day, the graffiti was gone. I don't know who got rid of it, but it really doesn't matter. In a way, they all did.

⋟ STEPS FOR EQUALITY ⋞

+ If you're an LGBT sports coach or an athlete, give the other athletes in your life the benefit of the doubt. Most people, especially young people, want to do the right thing. They just don't always know how to do it. Your coming out gives them an opportunity to step up to the plate.

+ If something "gay" comes up in conversation, address it. If not, don't force it. And remember, a little bit of humor goes a long way toward making straight people feel as comfortable as you are with your sexuality.

+ If you're not a coach, your support is still important. You can write a letter to the editor whenever a gay sports issue comes up; ask your college or high school athletic director what he or she is doing to support gay issues, or ask your favorite pro team to include domestic partners in their "Family Day" promotions.

Create the Space to Be
Out While About

Kelli O'Donnell, Founder, R Family Vacations

A couple of years ago, Rosie got a frantic phone call from our friend Gregg. Gregg was the vice president of a gay travel company whose all-gay cruise was scheduled to depart in a few days and the headline entertainer had just canceled. Gregg asked Rosie if she had any friends she could call for him at the last minute. To his surprise (and mine), she told him that we'd go on the cruise and she would perform.

While on the cruise, Rosie and I were moved by the incredible camaraderie—as well as all the fun and laughter—we witnessed among the gay passengers. When we got home, Rosie called Gregg and asked him if there were any cruises for gay and lesbian families. "Not yet," he replied. Rosie suggested that he and I create the company together, and R Family Vacations was born.

I've been asked many times why it's necessary to have vacations geared toward gay and lesbian families. In July 2004, on the first day of our first cruise, I walked out on the dock with my five-year-old son, Blake, to start checking our guests in. "Two mommies everywhere!" Blake shouted. I looked around at the arriving guests—gay and lesbian vacationers with their small children, parents, siblings, and friends—and saw the excited looks on everyone's face. From the moment we started sailing down the Hudson River, the mood on the ship was full of joy and the most amazing energy. For once, everyone was normal. Everyone was accepted. Everyone was welcome.

The trip was an eventful one. Cindi Love from the Dallas MCC Church performed 23 weddings. We had entertainment for adults and kids, as well as workshops on issues such as adoption and financial planning. And perhaps most important, we offered a space for our guests to be out without fears of judgment or intolerance. It was a vacation free from curious

CREATE AN EQUAL SOCIETY 141

stares and homophobic attitudes. And it was a rousing success: nearly half of our passengers immediately rebooked for the next summer's cruise. After the trip, we received lots of letters from parents who wrote about how much this cruise had affected their children's lives in such a positive way. One parent told us that her daughter had never told her friends that she had two moms. But after her experience on the cruise, she was proud of that fact.

Gay and lesbian travelers can face many awkward moments when we're on vacation: checking into a hotel with our partner and asking for one bed, sharing a romantic dinner, or watching the sunset and wanting to hold hands but hesitating because of the stares that might be directed our way. On our cruise, though, LGBT adults and their children can finally feel at ease—and what could be more relaxing than that?

⇒ STEPS FOR EQUALITY ⇐

+ Consider taking a lesbian- and gay-themed vacation. Some companies, like ours, welcome you to invite along your straight friends and family. It's a unique opportunity for the whole family to enjoy a vacation together, and for straight loved ones to take part in the joys of our community. Visit our website (www.rfamilyvacations.com) for more information.

+ Visit gay-friendly destinations, like Provincetown, Massachusetts (visit www.ptown.org for details on vacation planning).

+ Whether you're LGBT or straight, support gay-friendly businesses when you travel. For example, fly airlines that extend bereavement fares and the sharing of frequent flyer miles to same-sex couples, rent cars at agencies that waive extra-driver fees for committed couples, and patronize businesses that don't discriminate against their LGBT employees. Ask companies these questions when booking your travel, or search for gay-friendly businesses through the International Gay and Lesbian Travel Association (www.iglta.com).

Leverage Your Spending Power

Justin Nelson and Chance Mitchell, Cofounders,
National Gay & Lesbian Chamber of Commerce

We sit here today as gay Americans, used as a wedge issue in the last presidential election—our lives, our families, and our values distorted in an unholy effort to win votes. Our civil liberties and quest for equal justice under the law hang in the balance as our president decides whether or not to follow through on campaign promises to placate the few at the expense of the many. Time and again Congress has refused to pass hate crimes legislation and the Employment Non-Discrimination Act. LGBT Americans and our allies must continue our fight for equality. However, to win we must fight smarter.

As the cofounders of the National Gay & Lesbian Chamber of Commerce (NGLCC), we believe that our quest for equality must be fashioned in the economic terms that give us a level playing field, as we engage our adversaries in a civilized debate on the issues that matter most to all Americans: taxes, employment, education, health care, the ability to care for our loved ones in times of need, and the freedom to live our lives in the manner we so choose.

It is time to realize that if we cannot win over our detractors with the "because it's the right thing to do" argument, then we must use a new tactic that will make a difference. We need a message so vital to all concerned that it cannot be ignored by this White House or this Congress. What *does* matter most to the people who seek to send us to the proverbial back of the bus? What can we use to make inroads with political decision makers in Washington, leadership in corporate America, and in communities around the country?

For far too long, people in the LGBT community have been unwilling to use "economics" and "activism" in the same sentence, as if somehow the two are diametrically opposed and anyone who utters them together is a sellout. This is exactly the wrong approach. We must all do our part to give an economic value to our community. We too can participate in the pocketbook advocacy that holds so much power in our society and our government.

The NGLCC works with Congress on both LGBT issues and those issues of economic importance to our community and all Americans. By highlighting the successes of "Ma and Ma" and "Pa and Pa" shops across the country, we have set out to give an accurate picture of the contributions LGBT people make to the economy and the nation. In a country where money talks, we must put our dollars behind businesses and politicians who support our rights and acknowledge our community. By educating ourselves on where we spend our money (so that we spend it on businesses that enforce anti-discrimination policies, offer equal benefits to LGBT people, and stand up for our community), we can leverage our spending power ($610 billion in 2005[1]) to demand that we're treated as second-class citizens no longer.

Conventional methods of in-your-face activism and "do it because it's the right thing" arguments have served our community well over the past 20 years, but they have hit the saturation point with the general public. If businesses and our government won't give us our rights because it is the right thing to do, then we must convince them to do it because it is the smart business thing to do.

⇉ STEPS FOR EQUALITY ⇇

+ Join the NGLCC: strength in numbers tells America's decision makers that we mean business. Your support as a business owner (LGBT or allied), professional, or student allows us to start new chapters and lobby Congress and the White House.

+ Talk to your political representatives and your local newspapers, and explain that the LGBT community's spending power will be $600 billion in 2005 and that our immense contribution to the economy should be rewarded with equal protection and rights under our laws.

+ Use the NGLCC website (www.nglcc.org) to see which companies are not only marketing to the LGBT community, but also buying back from certified LGBT suppliers.

Grab the Brass Ring of Equality

Margaret Cho, Comedian

If we hold fast to our beliefs, what else can result but new standards for our elected officials? If gay and lesbian couples continue to line up at city halls all over the nation demanding marriage licenses; if one by one, the mayors decide to let the people have what rightly belongs to them; if the media sees these families (solid and loving, so many already in place for years and years, deserving acknowledgment from government agencies and society at large); if our opponents are unable to ignore the numbers of us willing to fight for what we believe in; if we can become an army of lovers—how could we lose this war?

We have no idea how powerful we actually are, and how much more powerful we can be. So many of us have not voted or even registered to vote. Understandably so, for we've never been considered part of the general, "respectable" population. Why vote in a country that cares so little about who we are? This land is your land, but this land isn't my land—that is what so many of us have come to believe. This second-class citizenship has sunk in so deeply that we have barely any awareness of it. We had no idea that this mindset is the enemy we are truly fighting.

Our silent complicity with the status quo—even alongside great strides in LGBT activism, and the emergence of mainstream gay icons from TV shows like *Will & Grace* and *Queer Eye for the Straight Guy*—has kept the true face of who we are hidden. We have no knowledge of how far our reach is. We don't know our own strength. We don't know that we are warriors. The time has come for us to know. Even if you are still in the closet, the voting booth is a private place to fight. No one has to know which side you are on but you, and know that when you are ready, you will be welcomed with open arms into your true family, the tribe you were born into.

If you are not gay, equality is still your issue, because if we lose this battle, who will be there to defend your rights? If the government is allowed to take freedoms away from a certain group of people, how much longer will it be until they come for you? We are a much more formidable opponent than anyone would have known. It's time to grab the brass ring of equality—the real civil union. How strong is your grip?

⋛ STEPS FOR EQUALITY ⋜

+ Stay informed and get involved. Visit my marriage equality resource (www.loveisloveislove.com) for petitions, news, and simple actions you can take to advance LGBT equality.

Endnotes

Section 4

1 C.J. Patterson, M. Fulcher, and J. Wainright. "Children of Lesbian and Gay Parents: Research, Law, and Policy." In B.L. Bottoms, M.B. Kovera, and B.D. McAuliff (Eds.), *Children, Social Science and the Law.* New York: Cambridge University Press. 2002. pp. 176-199.

2 J. C. Armesto J. C. "Developmental and Contextual Factors That Influence Gay Fathers' Parental Competence: A Review of the Literature." *Psychology of Men and Masculinity.* 3 (2002): pp. 67-78.
C.J. Patterson. "Family Relationships of Lesbians and Gay Men." *Journal of Marriage and Family.* 62 (2000): pp. 1052-1069.
F. Tasker and S. Golombok. *Growing Up in a Lesbian Family.* New York: Guilford Press. 1997.

3 J.J. Conger. Proceedings of the American Psychological Association, Incorporated, for the Year 1974: Minutes of the Annual Meeting of the Council of Representatives. *American Psychologist.* 30 (1975): pp. 620-651.
V.M. Mays and S.D. Cochran. "Mental Health Correlates of Perceived Discrimination among Lesbian, Gay, and Bisexual Adults in the United States. *American Journal of Public Health.* 91 (2001): pp. 1869-1876.
I.H. Meyer. "Prejudice, Social Stress, and Mental Health in Lesbian, Gay, and Bisexual Populations: Conceptual Issues and Research Evidence." *Psychological Bulletin.* 129 (2003): pp. 674-697.

4 C.J. Patterson. "Family Relationships of Lesbians and Gay Men." *Journal of Marriage and Family.* 62 (2000): pp. 1052-1069.
C.J. Patterson. "Lesbian and Gay Parents and Their Children: Summary of Research Findings." *Lesbian and Gay Parenting: A Resource for Psychologists.* Washington, DC: American Psychological Association. 2004.
E.C. Perrin and the Committee on Psychosocial Aspects of Child and Family Health. "Technical Report: Coparent or Second-Parent

Adoption by Same-Sex Parents." *Pediatrics.* 109 (2002): pp. 341-344.

5 C.J. Patterson. "Family Relationships of Lesbians and Gay Men." *Journal of Marriage and Family.* 62 (2000): pp. 1052-1069.
F. Tasker. "Children in Lesbian-Led Families: A Review." *Clinical Child Psychology and Psychiatry.* 4 (1999): pp. 153-166.

6 C.J. Patterson. "Family Relationships of Lesbians and Gay Men." *Journal of Marriage and Family.* 62 (2000): pp. 1052-1069.
C.J. Patterson. "Lesbian and Gay Parents and Their Children: Summary of Research Findings." *Lesbian and Gay Parenting: A Resource for Psychologists.* Washington, DC: American Psychological Association. 2004.

7 D. Flaks, I. Ficher, F. Masterpasqua, and G. Joseph. "Lesbians Choosing Motherhood: A Comparative Study of Lesbian and Heterosexual Parents and Their Children." *Developmental Psychology.* 31 (1995): pp. 104-114.

8 C.J. Patterson. "Lesbian and Gay Parents and Their Children: Summary of Research Findings." *Lesbian and Gay Parenting: A Resource for Psychologists.* Washington, DC: American Psychological Association. 2004.

9 C.J. Patterson. "Lesbian and Gay Parents and Their Children: Summary of Research Findings." *Lesbian and Gay Parenting: A Resource for Psychologists.* Washington, DC: American Psychological Association. 2004.

10 E.C. Perrin and the Committee on Psychosocial Aspects of Child and Family Health. "Technical Report: Coparent or Second-Parent Adoption by Same-Sex Parents." *Pediatrics.* 109 (2002): pp. 341-344.
J. Stacey and T.J. Biblarz. "(How) Does Sexual Orientation of Parents Matter?" *American Sociological Review.* 65 (2001): pp. 159-183.
F. Tasker. "Children in Lesbian-Led Families: A Review." *Clinical Child Psychology and Psychiatry.* 4 (1999): pp. 153-166.

11 C.J. Patterson. "Gay Fathers." In M.E. Lamb (Ed.), *The Role of the Father in Child Development.* New York: John Wiley. 2004.
"Ethical Principles of Psychologists and Code of Conduct." *American Psychologist.* 57 (2002): pp. 1060-1073.

12 C.J. Patterson. "Family Relationships of Lesbians and Gay Men."

Journal of Marriage and Family. 62 (2000): pp. 1052-1069.

C.J. Patterson. "Lesbian and Gay Parents and Their Children: Summary of Research Findings." *Lesbian and Gay Parenting: A Resource for Psychologists.* Washington, DC: American Psychological Association. 2004.

E.C. Perrin and the Committee on Psychosocial Aspects of Child and Family Health. "Technical Report: Coparent or Second-Parent Adoption by Same-Sex Parents." *Pediatrics.* 109 (2002): pp. 341-344.

J. Stacey and T.J. Biblarz. "(How) Does Sexual Orientation of Parents Matter?" *American Sociological Review.* 65 (2001): pp. 159-183.

F. Tasker. "Children in Lesbian-Led Families: A review." *Clinical Child Psychology and Psychiatry.* 4 (1999): pp. 153-166.

F. Tasker and S. Golombok. *Growing Up in a Lesbian Family.* New York: Guilford Press. 1997.

13 P.H. DeLeon. Proceedings of the American Psychological Association, Incorporated, for the Year 1992: Minutes of the Annual Meeting of the Council of Representatives, August 13 and 16, 1992, and February 26 to 28, 1993, Washington, D.C. *American Psychologist.* 48 (1993): p. 782.

P.H. DeLeon, Proceedings of the American Psychological Association, Incorporated, for the Year 1994: Minutes of the Annual Meeting of the Council of Representatives, August 11 and 14, 1994, Los Angeles, and February 17 to 19, 1995, Washington, D.C. *American Psychologist.* 49 (1995): pp. 627-628.

R.E. Fox. Proceedings of the American Psychological Association, Incorporated, for the Year 1990: Minutes of the Annual Meeting of the Council of Representatives, August 9 and 12, 1990, Boston, and February 8 to 9, 1991, Washington, D.C. *American Psychologist.* 45 (1991): p. 845.

R.F. Levant. Proceedings of the American Psychological Association, Incorporated, for the Legislative Year 1999: Minutes of the Annual Meeting of the Council of Representatives, February 19 to 21, 1999, Washington, D.C., and August 19 and 22, 1999, Boston; and Minutes of the February, June, August, and December 1999 Meetings of the Board of Directors. *American Psychologist.* 55 (2000): pp. 832-890.

14 J.J. Conger. Proceedings of the American Psychological
    Association, Incorporated, for the Year 1974: Minutes of the
    Annual Meeting of the Council of Representatives. *American
    Psychologist*. 30 (1975): pp. 620-651.
    "Ethical Principles of Psychologists and Code of Conduct."
    American Psychologist. 57 (2002): pp. 1060-1073.
15 *Lofton v. Secretary of Department of Children and Family Services*,
    358 F.3d 804 (11th Cir. 2004).
16 GLSEN National School Climate Survey. Available at:
    www.glsen.org/cgi-in/iowa/all/library/record/1413.html.
17 GLSEN State of the States Report. Available at: www.glsen.org/
    cgi-bin/iowa/all/library/record/1687.html.
18 B.N. Cochran, A.J. Stewart, J.A. Ginzler, and A.M. Cauce. 2002.
19 *Pediatrics* 101 (1998): pp. 895-902.
20 *Archives of Pediatric & Adolescent Medicine*. 153 (1999): pp. 487-
    493.

Section 5

1 *Legal Realities* (a Transgender Law Center report released in
   conjunction with the National Center for Lesbian Rights). 2002.
2 Department of Defense Survey. June 2000.
3 Department of Defense Survey. June 2000.

Section 6

1 National Institute for Mental Health. *Depression: A Treatable
   Illness*. NIH Publication No. 03-5299. March 2003.
2 U.S. Department of Health and Human Services. *Mental Health: A
   Report of the Surgeon General*. 1999.
3 See www.psych.org/public_info/homose~1.cfm, www.apa.org/
   pubinfo/answers.html, and www.socialworkers.org/pubs/news/
   2000/03/converting.htm.

Section 7

1 Witeck-Combs Communications.

Resources

COME TOGETHER ACROSS LINES OF DIFFERENCE

Organizations that support LGBT people of color, their loved ones, and their supporters include APIQWTC: Asian Pacific Islander Queer Women & Transgender Coalition (www.apiqwtc.org); APLBTN: Asian & Pacific Islander Lesbian, Bisexual, and Transgender Network (www.aplbtn.org); BAAITS: Bay Area American Indian Two-Spirits (www.baaits.org); The Black Stripe: The Internet's Leading Resource for News, Information, and Culture Affecting Lesbian, Gay, Bisexual, and Transgendered People of African Descent (www.blackstripe.com/blacklist); GAPA: Gay Asian Pacific Alliance (www.gapa.org); LLEGO: National Latino/a Lesbian, Gay, Bisexual, & Transgender Organization (www.llego.org); NABWMT: National Association of Black & White Men Together (www.nbwmt.org); NBJC: National Black Justice Coalition: Civil Rights for Everyone (www.nbj coalition.org).

WATCH MOVIES ABOUT LGBT LIFE

Read more about LGBT life on the silver screen in these books: *The Bent Lens: A World Guide to Gay and Lesbian Film* by Lisa Daniel and Claire Jackson (available through Alyson Publications at www.alyson.com); *Images in the Dark: An Encyclopedia of Gay and Lesbian Film and Video* by Raymond Murray (available through TLA Publications at www.tlavideo.com); and *The Ultimate Guide to Lesbian & Gay Film and Video*, edited by Jenni Olson (available through Serpent's Tail at www.ser pentstail.com).

TAKE A LESSON FROM HISTORY

For more information on queer history projects and to access LGBT archives, contact the Gay, Lesbian, Bisexual, Transgender Historical Society (www.glbthistory.org); the Gerber/Hart Library (www.gerberhart.org); the

Lesbian Herstory Archives (www.datalounge.net/network/pages/lha); the Northwest Lesbian and Gay History Museum Project (www.home.earth link.net/~ruthpett/lgbthistorynw); the Ohio Lesbian Archives (www.geoc ities.com/ohiolesbianarchives); and the ONE National Lesbian and Gay Archives (www.oneinstitute.org).

A number of documentaries offer a glimpse of LGBT history. These include *No Secret Anymore: The Times of Del Martin and Phyllis Lyon*, *The Times of Harvey Milk*, *Hope Along the Wind: The Life of Harry Hay*, *Tongues Untied*, and *The Cockettes*.

STAY THE COURSE ON MARRIAGE

Email action lists to join and organizations to support include the ACLU Lesbian and Gay Rights Project (www.aclu.org), Freedom to Marry (www.freedomtomarry.org), Gay & Lesbian Advocates & Defenders (www.glad.org), Lambda Legal (www.lambdalegal.org), and the National Center for Lesbian Rights (www.nclrights.org).

SUPPORT PARENTAL RIGHTS FOR BOTH PARENTS

Some organizations that work for equal rights for same-sex parents are the Human Rights Campaign (www.hrc.org), Lambda Legal Defense and Education Fund (www.lambdalegal.org), and the National Center for Lesbian Rights (www.nclrights.org).

ADDRESS TRANSGENDER RIGHTS

Look for these educational materials in the resource or publication sec-tion of the listed website: *Trans Realities* by the Transgender Law Center and the National Center for Lesbian Rights www.transgenderlawcen ter.org), *Transgender Equality: A Handbook for Activists and Policymakers* by the National Gay and Lesbian Task Force (www.thetaskforce.org), *Transgender Family Resources* by Children of Lesbians and Gays Everywhere (www.colage.org).

The following organizations, which fight for transgender rights, could use your support: the National Center for Transgender Equality (www.ncte quality.org), Sylvia Rivera Law Project (www.srlp.org), TGI Justice Project (www.tgijp.org), and the Transgender Law Center (www.transgender lawcenter.org).

To find LGBT-identified or LGBT-affirmative mental health professionals, contact the Association of Gay and Lesbian Psychiatrists (www.aglp.org) and the Association for Gay, Lesbian, and Bisexual Issues in Counseling (www.aglbic.org). Also, look for listings for psychiatrists and therapists in the Gay and Lesbian Yellow Pages (www.glyp.com) and through the Gay Lesbian International Therapist Search Engine (www.glitse.com). For more information on lesbian and gay health issues, look at www.gay health.com.

The following organizations can help you locate support groups in your area: Parents, Families and Friends of Lesbians and Gays (www.pflag.org); Transgender Forum (www.transgender.org); Bisexual Resource Center (www.biresource.org); and, for teens, the Gay, Lesbian, and Straight Education Network (www.glsen.org).

A number of self-help books written for LGBT people and their loved ones can help those suffering from depression or other psychological stress. These include: *Growth and Intimacy for Gay Men: A Workbook* by Christopher J. Alexander (Haworth Press, 1997); *Don't Call Me Nuts: Coping with the Stigma of Mental Illness* by Patrick Corrigan and Robert Lundin (Recovery Press, 2001); *The Lesbian Love Companion: How to Survive Everything from Heartthrob to Heartbreak* by Marny Hall (HarperSanFrancisco, 1998); *The Gay and Lesbian Self-Esteem Book: A Guide to Loving Ourselves* by Kimeron Hardin (New Harbinger, 1999); *Queer Blues: The Lesbian and Gay Guide to Overcoming Depression* by Kimeron Hardin and Marny Hall (New Harbinger, 2001); *Coming Out of Shame: Transforming Gay and Lesbian Lives* by Gershen Kaufman and Lev Raphael (Broadway, 1996); and *Accepting Ourselves and Others: A Journey into Recovery from Addictive and Compulsive Behavior for Gays, Lesbians, and Bisexuals* by Sheppard Kominars and Kathryn Kominars (Hazleden, 1996).

ADVOCATE FOR OUR ELDERS

Locate local and national resources for LGBT elders, and find out how to volunteer to support our elders at www.sageusa.org.

Learn more about what it's like to grow old in the LGBT community in these books: *Village Elders* by Penny Coleman (University of Illinois

Press, 2000); and *Midlife & Aging in Gay America*, edited by D. Kimmel and D. Martin (Harrington Park Press, 2002).

KEEP THE FAITH

You can find a number of spiritual resources on the web, no matter what your affiliation. The Other Side (www.theotherside.org/resources /gay/links.html) offers links to more than 60 LGBT faith groups. Also, the following organizations can provide support for LGBT people in Christianity, Judaism, and Islam, respectively: Metropolitan Community Churches (www.mcchurch.org), GayJews.org (www.members. tripod.com/~djs28), and the Al-Fatiha Foundation (www.al-fatiha.org). To read more about LGBT spirituality, look up these titles: *Our Tribe, Too: Queer Folks, God, Jesus and the Bible* by Rev. Elder Nancy Wilson (HarperSanFrancisco, 1995); *Gay Theology without Apology* by Gary D. Comstock (Pilgrim Press, 1993); *Steps to Recovery from Bible Abuse* by Rev. Dr. Rembert Truluck (Chio Rho Press, 2000), and *Coming Out Spiritually: The Next Step* by Christian De La Huerta (Jeremy Tarcher, 1999).

Contributors

Tomas Almaguer is currently a visiting scholar at the Center for Latino Policy Research and the Ethnic Studies Department at the University of California at Berkeley. He is the author of *Racial Fault Lines: The Historical Origins of White Supremacy in California* and "Chicano Men: A Cartography of Homosexual Identity and Behavior."

Clinton Anderson—who serves as the Lesbian, Gay, and Bisexual Concerns Officer for the American Psychological Association (APA)—adapted this essay from the APA Resolution on Sexual Orientation, Parents, and Children, adopted in 2004. The full policy resolution can be accessed from www.apa.org/pi/lgbc/homepage.html.

Caryn Aviv, Ph.D., is codirector of Mosaic: The National Jewish Center for Sexual and Gender Diversity and a lecturer in Judaic studies and sociology at the University of Denver. She is coauthor of *Queer Jews, New Jews: The End of the Jewish Diaspora*, and the forthcoming *Queer in America: Then and Now*.

Diane Anderson-Minshall is the executive editor of *Curve* magazine as well as the cofounder and former publisher of *Alice* magazine and the cofounder and former editor of *Girlfriends* magazine. Her writing has appeared in *Passport, Bust, Bitch, Seventeen, Venus, Teenage, Utne Reader, The Advocate, Diva*, and more. She was a 2004 George Washington Williams fellow.

Julia Bloch is the managing editor of *Curve* magazine (www.curvemag.com), a cofounder of Bigfan Press (www.bigfanpress.com), and a poet who lives in San Francisco, where she awaits the next wedding revolution and writes epistolary poems to Kelly Clarkson, the tow-headed winner of the first *American Idol*.

Mary L. Bonauto is the Civil Rights Project director for Gay & Lesbian Advocates & Defenders (www.glad.org), an organization dedicated to ending discrimination based on sexual orientation, HIV status, and gender identity and expression. Bonauto's precedent-setting cases have established equal marriage in Massachusetts and civil unions in Vermont.

Dulce Reyes Bonilla is a graduate student in Sociology on her way to law school. She is a long-term activist in the LGBT people of color and immigrant rights communities and has written on issues relevant to both. A "transnational Brooklynite", she is most recently published in an anthology on Dominicanness and intra-group marginalization.

Craig A. Bowman is the executive director of the National Youth Advocacy Coalition (www.nyacyouth.org). NYAC fights injustice against LGBT youth and advocates for their physical and emotional well-being, so that LGBT youth of all races, ethnicities, class backgrounds, and gender identities live to their fullest potential.

Kevin M. Cathcart, executive director of Lambda Legal since 1992, is a leading strategist and spokesperson in the movement to achieve full civil rights for LGBT people and those with HIV. Under Cathcart's leadership, Lambda Legal promotes security, respect, and fairness for all people regardless of sexual orientation, gender identity, or HIV status.

Debra Chasnoff is an Academy Award–winning documentary filmmaker whose films have been catalysts for social change. *It's Elementary—Talking About Gay Issues in School* has inspired millions of viewers to rethink their assumptions about whether to talk to kids about gay people. For a full list of her films, including *That's a Family!*, see www.womedia.org.

Comedian **Margaret Cho** has launched three successful national tours in the past five years, turning each into a concert film. Always incorporating activism in her comedy, Cho has been honored by the ACLU, NOW, the National Gay and Lesbian Task Force, and the Asian American Legal Defense and Education Fund for her efforts to promote equal rights for all in her work. Visit her online at MargaretCho.com.

Matt Coles is the author of *Try This at Home: A Do-It-Yourself Guide to Winning Lesbian and Gay Rights* and has been director of the ACLU's Lesbian and Gay Rights and HIV/AIDS Project since 1995. The project works toward equal treatment for LGBT people and an end to discrimination in the public and private sectors.

Steven Cozza (www.stevencozza.com), 19, is currently training in Europe to become a world-class cyclist. During the off-season, he continues to be a spokesperson for Scouting for All (www.scoutingforall.org), the organization he founded at age 12 with his father.

Christopher Daley is an attorney with the Transgender Law Center (www.transgenderlawcenter.org), a California-based organization that works with transgender community members and their families, attorneys, activists, and allies to overcome gender-identity bias and discrimination.

Tina D'Elia and **Andy Wong** are staff members at Community United Against Violence (www.cuav.org), an LGBT anti-violence group based in San Francisco. CUAV's 24-hour crisis line is (415) 333-HELP. CUAV welcomes monetary support as well as local volunteers to participate as peer counselors on the crisis line or with the Speaker's Bureau; call (415) 777-5500 for more information.

Diva Dan is originally from Tennessee and now resides in California with her partner of 13 years. She considers herself to be a human being, above all things, as well as an activist, artist, and drag queen extraordinaire. For a more titillating glimpse into the outrageous life of Diva Dan, log onto www.divadan.com.

Emily Doskow is a Nolo Press author and editor, and a mediator and attorney in private practice in Berkeley, California. She specializes in adoption and family mediation, especially for same-sex couples.

Joan M. Garry is the former executive director of the Gay & Lesbian Alliance Against Defamation (GLAAD), which is dedicated to promoting the fair, accurate, and inclusive representation of LGBT people in the media. For more information about GLAAD's efforts to end discrimination based on gender identity and sexual orientation, visit www.glaad.org.

Candace Gingrich is the youth outreach manager and the former National Coming Out Project manager for the Human Rights Campaign (www.hrc.org). She's also the author of the 1996 autobiography *The Accidental Activist*, which chronicles her involvement in the movement for LGBT equal rights.

Joel Ginsberg is the executive director of the Gay and Lesbian Medical Association (www.glma.org). For more than 20 years, GLMA has been working to ensure equality in health care for LGBT people, through professional education, public policy work, patient education and referrals, and the promotion of research.

Jerry Greenfield is the cofounder of Ben & Jerry's Ice Cream. He met his business partner, Ben Cohen, when they were two of the widest students at Calhoun High in Merrick, Long Island. In 1978, after receiving A's in a correspondence course in ice cream making, he and Ben set up their first Ben & Jerry's ice cream parlor in Burlington, Vermont.

Kimeron Hardin, Ph.D., is a psychologist in the San Francisco Bay Area. He is the author of *The Gay and Lesbian Self-Esteem Book: A Guide to Loving Ourselves* and coauthor (with Marny Hall, Ph.D.) of *Queer Blues: The Lesbian and Gay Guide to Overcoming Depression.*

Scott J. Hamilton is deputy executive director of SAGE (Services and Advocacy for GLBT Elders), the country's oldest and largest community-based organization devoted to LGBT seniors. Scott makes his home in Brooklyn, New York, with his partner Wayne Johnson of 14 years.

Daisy Hernández is a writer and editor for *ColorLines* magazine and coeditor of the feminist anthology *Colonize This!*. She has written a column for *Ms.* magazine and reported for the *New York Times*. Her essays have been published in several anthologies including *Without a Net* and *Border-Line Personalities*. She is Cuban and Colombian and lives in California with her cat Zami.

Frederick Hertz is a practicing attorney in Oakland, California. He is the author of *Legal Affairs: Essential Advice for Same-Sex Couples* and coauthor of *A Legal Guide for Lesbian & Gay Couples.*

Thea Hillman is an activist, performer, and writer. Her latest book, *For Lack of a Better Word*, will be released in 2006. For more information, visit www.theahillman.com.

Noelle Howey is the author of *Dress Codes*, which won the American Library Association's Gay & Lesbian Book Award and a Lambda Literary Award, and was selected for the *Good Morning, America!* book club. She also edited the award-winning anthology *Out of the Ordinary*, about the children of gay, lesbian, and transgender parents.

Sue Hyde launched the National Gay and Lesbian Task Force's Privacy Project in 1986 and now directs the annual Creating Change Conference. Founded in 1973, the NGLTF was the first national civil rights and advocacy organization for LGBT people. It continues to work toward building grassroots political strength.

Kevin Jennings is the founder and executive director of the Gay, Lesbian, and Straight Education Network (www.glsen.org). A former high school history teacher, he has written five books, including *Always My Child: A Parent's Guide to Understanding Your Gay, Lesbian, Bisexual, Transgender or Questioning Son or Daughter*.

Kate Kendell is the executive director of the National Center for Lesbian Rights, a national legal advocacy organization focused on achieving full justice and equality for lesbians and all others marginalized by discrimination based on sexual orientation or gender identity.

Terence Kissack is the executive director of the Gay, Lesbian, Bisexual, Transgender Historical Society. He has written a number of articles and reviews and is currently revising his dissertation, *Anarchism and the Politics of Homosexuality*, for publication. He can be reached at terence@glbthistory.org.

Victoria Neilson is the legal director of Immigration Equality, a national grassroots organization that advocates for equality for LGBT and HIV-positive individuals under U.S. immigration law. She has also been the litigation director of the HIV Law Project.

Justin Nelson and **Chance Mitchell** are the cofounders of the National Gay & Lesbian Chamber of Commerce. The NGLCC represents the interests of the estimated 800,000 to 1.2 million LGBT-owned businesses and LGBT entrepreneurs. To learn more, visit www.nglcc.org or email info@nglcc.org.

Nathaniel Obler first got involved in COLAGE at Family Week, an annual weeklong event in Provincetown, Massachusetts, and now serves on the COLAGE board of directors. Founded in 1990 by a group of "queerspawn,"

COLAGE offers support, information, and workshops to children of queer parents.

Kelli O'Donnell, cofounder of R Family Vacations, is also executive director of Rosie's Broadway Kids, a fully funded arts program for New York City public schools that serve primarily disadvantaged students. A former Nickelodeon marketing executive, she is married to entertainer Rosie O'Donnell, with whom she has four young children.

C. Dixon Osburn is the executive director of Servicemembers Legal Defense Network, a national, nonprofit legal services, watchdog, and policy organization dedicated to ending discrimination against military personnel affected by the "Don't Ask, Don't Tell" policy.

The Reverend **Dr. Troy D. Perry** is the founder of Metropolitan Community Churches, the world's largest faith group with an affirming ministry to LGBT people. He is the author of four books, including *The Lord Is My Shepherd and He Knows I'm Gay* and *Ten Spiritual Truths for Successful Living for Gays And Lesbians* (*And Everyone Else!*). Email him at info@MCCchurch.org.

Keely Savoie is a freelance writer based in Brooklyn, New York. She writes a column for InTheFray.com and frequently contributes to *Bitch* magazine, where she serves as the queer media watchdog. She welcomes your comments and feedback at BurningPen@gmail.com.

William F. Schulz, D.Min., former president of the Unitarian Universalist Association of Congregations, has been executive director of Amnesty International USA since 1994. The organization's OUTfront Program includes more than 13,000 members in the United States and is part of a global network working to stop human rights abuses against LGBT people.

Judy Shepard is founder and executive director of the Matthew Shepard Foundation (www.matthewshepard.org).

Arlene Stein is an associate professor of sociology at Rutgers University. Her latest book is *The Stranger Next Door: The Story of a Small Community's Battle over Sex, Faith, and Civil Rights*, about a group of religious conser-

160

vatives whose stance on gay rights polarized a small town. She has also written *Sex and Sensibility: Stories of a Lesbian Generation.*

Renate Stendhal (www.renatestendhal.com) is a German-born writer, writing coach, and spiritual/psychological counselor who works in Berkeley and San Francisco, California. Her books include *Sex and Other Sacred Games* (with her partner, Kim Chernin) and, most recently, *True Secrets of Lesbian Desire: Keeping Sex Alive in Long-Term Relationships.*

Anne Stockwell is senior arts and entertainment editor of *The Advocate*, a national gay and lesbian news magazine. A frequent public commentator on LGBT issues, she is the author of *The Guerrilla Guide to Mastering Student Loan Debt* and the founder of MoneyPants.com, the first online personal finance community for women.

Johnny Symons is the director and producer of the Emmy-nominated documentary *Daddy & Papa* (www.daddyandpapa.com), which chronicles the personal, cultural, and political journeys of four families headed by gay men, including his own. He can be reached at johnny@johnnysy mons.com.

Craig E. Thompson is executive director of AIDS Project Los Angeles (APLA). One of the largest nonprofit AIDS service organizations in the country, APLA provides bilingual direct services, prevention education, and leadership on HIV/AIDS-related policy and legislation. Founded by four friends in 1982, APLA is a community-based, volunteer-supported organization with local, national and global reach. For more information, visit www.apla.org http://www.apla.org/.

Samuel Thoron is the national president of PFLAG. He and his wife, Julia, who live in the San Francisco Bay Area, are the proud parents of two straight sons and a lesbian daughter.

Leland Traiman, R.N., is a family nurse practitioner who founded the gay sperm bank Rainbow Flag Health Services (www.gayspermbank.com). He also chaired Berkeley's Domestic Partner Task Force, crafting America's first domestic partner policy. In his domestic life, he is known as Stewart's husband and Julian's papa, and is a known donor to Isa.

Named by *Time* magazine as one of 50 influential American leaders under 40, **Rebecca Walker** is the author of the international bestseller *Black, White and Jewish: Autobiography of a Shifting Self*; the editor of *What Makes a Man* and *To Be Real: Telling the Truth and Changing the Face of Feminism*; and a cofounder of the Third Wave Foundation.

The Reverend **Dr. D. Mark Wilson** is an ordained American Baptist Minister and a former pastor. He has also earned a Ph.D. in sociology. He is currently an assistant professor in ministry and congregational leadership at the Pacific School of Religion and a lecturer in the Department of Sociology at the University of California, Berkeley.

Dan Woog (www.danwoog.com), the head soccer coach at Staples High School in Westport, Connecticut, was the 1990 National Youth Soccer Coach of the Year. He is also the author of 14 books, including *Jocks: True Stories of America's Gay Male Athletes* and *Jocks 2: Coming Out to Play*.

Acknowledgments

Math has never been my strong suit. Normally I don't count this among my blessings. But it came in handy, for once, the day publisher Karen Bouris asked me if I'd like to edit this book. Fifty essays written by 50 gay rights activists? Great idea! No problem! Six months and 60,000 inviting, cajoling, entreating, groveling, and desperate phone calls and emails later, it occurred to me that 50 is in fact a fairly large number of essays to solicit, collect, and edit into a cohesive whole—an unattainable goal, I'm certain, were it not for the efforts of those who made this book possible.

First among them, the recipients of those phone calls and emails: the organizations and individuals who stopped the crucial work they were doing long enough to write the compelling, moving, hilarious, poignant essays that comprise this book.

Next in the category of "couldn't have done it without them": the Inner Ocean Publishing team. Publisher Karen Bouris incited, inspired, and held fast to the book's purpose and spirit. At every crossroads, Karen's intelligence, integrity, and good cheer lit the way. Associate Editor Alma Bune was the steady hand at the wheel. Sales and marketing director Mark Kerr, publicity manager Katie McMillan, and publicist Gail Leondar-Wright invested huge stores of creativity and determination to ensure that this book is available to those who need it—and those who might not otherwise know that they do. Special mention must also be made of the indomitable, inimitable "Friend of Inner Ocean," Ms. Kimberly Burns.

Angela Watrous, my coeditor, did for this book what has been accurately described as the "heavy lifting." She edited every essay, managed to make 50 *very* individual points of view conform to a unique and demanding format, and argued vociferously for this book's best interests at every turn. Working with Angela has been a learning experience I count myself fortunate to have had.

Amy Rennert, my agent, first made the match, then provided the level of encouragement, support, wisdom, and enthusiasm I've become spoiled enough, as her longtime client, to expect. Speaking of spoiled: my lovely wife, Katrine Thomas, provided life-sustaining vinaigrette as well as too many delicious delights, earthly and otherwise, to mention. My sons, Jesse Graham and Peter Graham, are—now and always—the two best reasons I have for insisting on a better world.

—*Meredith Maran*

A tremendous amount of time and energy went into this collection. Inner Ocean Publisher Karen Bouris conceived of the idea—born from a tremendous commitment to social change and a steadfast belief in the power of books—and she helped shape the project all along the way. Working with Karen and editorial diva Alma Bune on Inner Ocean's Action Guide series is one of my great pleasures in life.

My coeditor Meredith Maran's intelligent perspective, vibrant personality, and astounding perseverance allowed her to round up an impressive array of contributors and leave her distinctive mark on this book. Before we embarked on this project, our paths crossed in many extraordinary ways, without our knowing it at the time. Fate was pushing us together, rightly telling us that our combined perspectives would lead to a better book than either of us could do alone.

Copyeditor extraordinaire Valerie Sinzdak worked her magic on each of these pages. We were lucky to have such a talented writer and editor at our disposal. I'm even more fortunate to be able to call her the love of my life.

Marketing and publicity geniuses Mark Kerr, Katie McMillan, and Gail Leondar-Wright have used the best of their big brains to deliver this labor of love into the world. And now it's in your hands, dear reader. Thank you for your desire to learn and for your commitment to equality. Take this book and run with it.

—*Angela Watrous*

About the Editors

Meredith Maran is the bestselling author of *DIRTY, Class Dismissed, Ben & Jerry's Double Dip,* and *What It's Like to Live Now.* She also wrote *Notes from an Incomplete Revolution* and a children's book, *How Would You Feel If Your Dad Was Gay?* Meredith writes for magazines and newspapers including *Health, Vibe, Salon.com, Self, Parenting, Utne Reader, Mother Jones,* the *San Francisco Chronicle,* and the *San Jose Mercury-News.* She was a founding editor of the gay and lesbian national magazine *Out/Look* and is currently the staff writer for UCLA's Center for Community Health on family issues.

Angela Watrous is the the editor of *Bare Your Soul,* a diverse anthology of personal essays discussing the intersection of spirituality with gender, sexuality, and race. She's the author of *Talk to Me* and *Love Tune-Ups,* as well as the advice column "Kiss and Tell," which is featured on www.planetout.com. Visit www.angelawatrous.com to learn more about Angela's work or contact her regarding speaking engagements.